Not My Will,
but Thine

Not My Will, but Thine

NEAL A. MAXWELL

DESERET
BOOK

SALT LAKE CITY, UTAH

First printing in hardbound 1988
First printing in paperbound 2008

Visit us at DeseretBook.com

Library of Congress Catalog Card Number: 88-71858

ISBN 0-88494-672-X (hardbound)
ISBN 978-1-59038-875-4 (paperbound)

Printed in the United States of America
Publishers Printing, Salt Lake City, UT

10   9   8   7   6   5   4   3

Contents

Acknowledgments

As always, I have not worked alone.

My gratitude is expressed to Elizabeth Haglund, who helped me when things were in a formative stage. Similarly, my appreciation is expressed to Dan Ludlow for his specific suggestions. Luke Ong was kind enough, once again, to provide computer runs on relevant scriptures. Susan Jackson not only typed this manuscript but also made valuable suggestions. Richard Turley and Grant Anderson graciously supplied some needed historical material. Elder Marion D. Hanks, without knowing it, enriched the manuscript by earlier gospel conversations. George Bickerstaff, an excellent editor, was especially helpful, and Cory Maxwell, while a supportive son, cared enough to be candid in his gentle suggestions.

This is not an official Church publication. Hence, even though I was helped in its preparation, I alone am responsible for the views it expresses.

1

"As Obedient Children"

In today's society, at the mere mention of the words *obedience* and *submissiveness* hackles rise and people are put on nervous alert. These virtues are unfashionable because many quickly assume them to be a threat to one's independence and agency. People promptly furnish examples from secular history to illustrate how obedience to unwise authority and servility to bad leaders have caused much human misery and suffering. It is difficult, therefore, to get a hearing for what the words *obedience* and *submissiveness* really mean—even when the clarifying phrase, "to God," is attached.

We are well conditioned indeed.

Yet such guardedness would be unseemly for disciples of Christ, who should be "willing to submit," this being a major quality inherent in saintliness, as King Benjamin doubly declared (Mosiah 3:19). Ironically, he who constitutes the greatest real threat to our freedom knows well how to fabricate and put us on guard against false and imagined threats. It is worth noting too that, even at the secular level, so much of society's functioning depends finally upon our civil obedience to the unenforceable. Whether in taking our turns at an intersection with "all-way" stop signs, or in giving compassionate service to the poor, we do not depend upon enforcing policemen. Obviously, ambivalence about authority has made us moderns unnoticing gulpers when it comes to swallowing a camel while straining at a gnat.

Spiritual submissiveness, a freely given obedience to God's purposes, is neither docility nor ignorant compliance. "As obedient children" (1 Peter 1:14) we are seeking to become more like our Heavenly Father. Yielding to Him, therefore, indicates neither disdain for life nor fatalistic resignation. Instead it is progressive participation in a very demanding discipleship.

This partnership with God, among other things, requires us to develop enough faith to repent and enough submissiveness to make and keep covenants, including temple covenants. Such faithful discipleship, however, would not be possible without prophets and scriptures to provide truths, doctrines, and answers sufficient to produce the strong faith needed. If we were without these firm and sure sources, doubt would prevail and insufficiency of individual intent would result. The basic human questions about identity and life's meaning would become unanswered screams of despair.

It is the Restoration scriptures (the Book of Mormon, the Doctrine and Covenants, the Pearl of Great Price, the Joseph Smith Translation of the Bible) which supply answers in such abundance to all the great questions. They bring us the nourishing richness of the Restoration gospel with its clarifying and reassuring messages from God to all His children. Greater faith and greater submissiveness result from hearing these answers and reassurances. Through them we are helped in many ways that are crucial to our salvation.

We are helped immeasurably to know that God really is a loving, Father God, not a distant cosmic presence.

We are helped immensely, too—whether by experiences, scriptures, temples, or living prophets—by being taught the plain and simple truths of the plan of salvation, including those about our true identity and real destiny.

We are helped by receiving worthily the reminding and saving ordinances and covenants.

We are helped by a Church which is established "for the perfecting of the saints" (Ephesians 4:12), especially since we have been instructed to become like the Father and the Son (Matthew 5:48; 3 Nephi 12:48; 27:27). When anciently the Lord used the phrase, "These I will make my rulers" (Abraham 3:23), those thus called were spirits who, even in their premortal state, were already becoming much like Him.

We are helped by having added scriptures such as the Book of Mormon to establish further the truths of the Holy Bible, and as another witness that God lives and that Jesus is the resurrected Lord and Savior of mankind.

We are helped as well by sensing, even finitely, the remarkable majesty and scope of God's work throughout the universe.

Finally, while pursuing our individual submissiveness, we are helped immensely when we ponder the infinite Atonement. God did not spare His Beloved Son from the anguish of these perfecting experiences. Jesus Christ has been, is, and will be our empathic Advocate with the Father. Not only is He our Advocate, but He helps us through our individual ordeals. By His own suffering He was perfected, including in His capacity to help us with our individual suffering (Alma 7:11–12).

At any suggestion that we submit our will to that of another human being, caution is certainly appropriate—indeed, we are not to "trust in the arm of flesh" (D&C 1:19). But our relationship to God is in this respect unlike that of mortal to mortal. We submit to God because He is God. We may safely and rationally do so because He is perfect—perfect in the attributes of love, mercy, justice, knowledge, patience, and so on. Moreover, his disciples have "proved Him in days that are past"; nor are they so provincial as to think that His work with mortals on this planet is God's first experience at redeeming.

Even though He is God, is each of us really willing to yield to His perfect love and omniscience? In addition to Jesus' perfect example, others have shown the way.

Obedient Adam sacrificed, saying, "I know not [why], save the Lord commanded me" (Moses 5:6). Submissive Abraham departed for a place of inheritance, going "out not knowing whither he went" (Hebrews 11:8). Trusting Nephi went back to Jerusalem for the vital brass plates, saying, "I will go and do the things which the Lord hath commanded, for I know . . . he shall prepare a way" (1 Nephi 3:7).

But as the Prophet Joseph observed, there are a "great many . . . too wise to be taught."[1] The knees of the mind bend so reluctantly.

Our discipleship is to be patterned after that of the Master (2 Nephi 31:16–17), who "learned . . . obedience by the things which he suffered" (Hebrews 5:8). Can we expect it to be otherwise with us? We who are entreated to take His yoke upon us (Matthew 11:29) cannot expect immunity from tutoring and suffering at the hands of a loving Father.

Faith is strongest when it is without illusions. Realistic faith alone provides allowance for the testing and proving dimensions of this mortal experience (D&C 98:12; Abraham 3:25). We undergo afflictions such as are "common to man" (1 Corinthians 10:13). Additionally, God will deliberately give us further lessons and experience which take us beyond the curriculum common to man and on into uncommon graduate studies or even post-doctoral discipleship. These trials are often the most difficult to bear. Our Father is full of pressing, tutorial love: "The Lord seeth fit to chasten his people; yea, he trieth their patience and their faith" (Mosiah 23:21). Nevertheless we are assured that "all these things shall give [us] experience, and shall be for [our] good," if we endure them well and learn from them (D&C 122:7; 121:8). For we are to learn much by our own experience.

Thus life itself does not do all of the inflicting. Indeed, some trials come directly from God or with His assent. On the final record will be the incontestable evidence as to whether we are "willing to submit to all things which the Lord seeth fit to inflict upon [us], even as a child doth submit to his father" (Mosiah 3:19).

Having taken his yoke upon us, then, we will experience—though on our small and lesser scale—certain things which permit us to learn of Jesus: loving when our love is not reciprocated or is even rejected, as with the wicked in His day; serving when our service is not appreciated, as with the nine lepers (Luke 17:12–19); seeing erring loved ones who are free to choose but who are choosing unwisely, as when He lamented, "O, Jerusalem . . ." (Matthew 23:37); watching in some the root of bitterness spring up to trouble and defile others (Hebrews 12:15); experiencing anguish as a result of what is happening to us and around us, but, as with Nephi, still knowing that God loves us (1 Nephi 11:17); being mocked and despised by the world, perhaps even betrayed, and feeling aloneness—all part of suffering in order to learn obedience (Hebrews 5:8).

The Prophet Joseph Smith taught that "all will suffer until they obey Christ himself."[2] Indeed, some suffering actually comes in striving to become like Christ as well as in obeying Him.

For true believers, then, life is a process of getting grounded spiritually: "Settle this in your hearts, that you will do the things which I shall teach, and command you" (JST, Luke 14:28).

Paul spoke of more than his own suffering in observing that "no chastening for the present seemeth to be joyous, but grievous" (Hebrews 12:11). We are not expected to pretend it is pleasant. Only *afterward* is "the peaceable fruit of righteousness" enjoyed by those who "are exercised thereby." In the Greek rendition, "exercised" is "trained, disciplined." Moroni said that only "*after* the trial of [our] faith" do we receive certain assurances and blessings (Ether 12:6, emphasis added). The developmental dues of discipleship must be paid *before* all of the blessings are received (D&C 130:20).

We cannot plan our own lives wisely unless we know about Heavenly Father's plan, including His commitment to the agency of His children. When we understand the plan, we can pursue participative and intelligent discipleship in the context of our inherent right to choose. Jesus chose in the premortal council whether He would be the Great Volunteer, and later whether He would undergo the tremendous rigors of the mortal Messiahship and the agonies of the Atonement, laying down His life voluntarily. We too must choose—sometimes among vexing alternatives but always with consequences.

In this mortal process all individuals have great worth, but not all individuals make equally worthwhile choices. The significance of this fact is that, while we are free to choose, we are not free to alter the consequences of our choices. We may decide merely to play at life, but that will not affect the seriousness of the immutable realities, the ordering principles, laws, and truths that are at work in the universe. We are free to pursue wrong courses, but we cannot shield ourselves from the attending consequences.

Wise choices, therefore, can best be made in the context of obedience to God's plan. The very notion of such obedience, such submission of will, however, is unpopular in this age of anti-authority. Increasing numbers of people think they live in an "unsponsored universe," in an "empire of chance" wherein mortals experience the "trampling march of unconscious power."[3] Some who accept this philosophy say, "Why should I obey anyone?"

Some disbelievers, decent and fine people, have genuinely and sincerely concluded there is no God. They feel He has not made Himself sufficiently known—at least on their terms. Trusting the intellect and the five senses, such persons learn little "of things as they really are, and of things as they really will be" (Jacob 4:13).

Still others prefer philosophical complexity to the simple gospel declarations. Each time Jesus or His prophets say "This is my gospel," the brief declaration implies a loving Heavenly Father who has sent His Only Begotten Son to rescue and redeem mankind. "And now, behold, I say unto you: This is the plan of salvation unto all men, through the blood of mine Only Begotten, who shall come in the meridian of time" (Moses 6:62; see also 3 Nephi 27:13, 20–21; D&C 76:40–42, 50). Yet some people reject this simple truth, seeking instead things they cannot understand. Theirs is a mistake of reckoning involving more than a few degrees on life's compass. It is an enormous error resulting from "looking beyond the mark" (Jacob 4:14)—the mark of Christ, who is at the center of it all.

As George MacDonald wisely wrote, "The one principle of hell is, I am my own!"[4] Fierce pride usually protects this wrong perception.

There are those who are exceedingly anxious to proclaim, "I did it my way!" Such selfish assertions are seen by some as a validation of individuality, while obedience to God is seen as a lessening of self. Yet obedience to God is really what makes the flowering of the full self possible. Otherwise—if every individual does only that which is right in his own eyes, unconnected with a sure standard of measure—the outcome will be sadness (Judges 21:25; D&C 1:16). In the forlorn conclusion of one drama, a final lamentation is expressed: "Are all men's lives . . . broken . . . why can't people have what they want? The things were all there to content everybody, yet everybody got the wrong thing. I don't know. It's beyond me. It's all darkness."[5]

Some say there are absolutely no absolutes, further encouraging each individual to "do his own thing" regardless; they do not realize that there is an emerging pattern after all. Those who wrongly and heedlessly do their own thing are really doing Lucifer's thing in an unconscious pattern of sobering servility. Men are that they might have joy, but Satan desires that all be miserable like unto himself (2 Nephi 2:25, 27). God desires true human happiness; it is the object and design of our existence, said Joseph Smith.[6] All blessings, however, come by obedience to the laws upon which happiness is predicated (D&C 130:20–21).

For all that, though, as we have already noted, life is not intended to be lived in an idyllic Eden. Spiritual submissiveness includes our acceptance of the ups and downs of life. We experience a mix of these universal challenges individually. Routine and general though they be, coping with routine afflictions requires real faith, for faith is needed daily and not only for extremity.

It takes faith, too, and obedience, to conquer selfishness, that unsubmissive characteristic which, if unchecked, produces profound personal melancholy and solitariness. Selfishness is a form of self-worship, and we have been told, "Thou shalt have *no* other Gods before me" (Exodus 20:3; emphasis added).

Many pursue this life as did those in Korihor's culture, wherein people believed that they fared in this life according to a pattern in which everyone "prospered according to his genius" and "conquered according to his strength." Furthermore, whatsoever was done in that Darwinistic process "was no crime" (Alma 30:17).

Clearly, the worldly living epitomized by such a philosophy celebrates openly the selfish doing of one's own thing. Its conformity masquerades as individuality—a circumstance somewhat like goldfish in a bowl congratulating themselves on their self-sufficiency while unacknowledging of the one who puts in the food pellets and changes the water.

Those of us favored with an understanding of essential gospel truths are, therefore, so greatly blessed. We are further blessed when Father imparts to us "the mysteries of God," including temple blessings. He is a very careful Father, however, for He "doth grant unto the children of men, according to the heed and diligence which they have given unto him" (Alma 12:9).

This process of merited, metered, divine disclosure has been under way from the very beginning.

> God had appointed that these things should come unto man, . . .
>
> Therefore he sent angels to converse with them, who caused men to behold of his glory.
>
> And they began from that time forth to call on his name; therefore God conversed with men, and made known unto them the plan of redemption, which had been prepared from the foundation of the world; and this he made known unto them according to their faith and repentance and their holy works (Alma 12:28–30).

Furthermore, the light of Christ is present in us mortals if we will respond to its illuminations (John 1:9; D&C 84:46).

In her introduction to *Anne of Green Gables*, Lucy Maude

Montgomery writes: "It has always seemed to me, ever since early childhood, amid all the commonplaces of life, I was very near to a kingdom of ideal beauty. Between it and me hung only a thin veil. I could never draw it quite aside, but sometimes a wind fluttered it and I caught a glimpse of the enchanting realm beyond—only a glimpse—but those glimpses have always made life worthwhile."[7]

But despite our innate longings for the ideally good and beautiful, it is so easy to be caught up instead in the cares and things of the world. This is done to our cost, however, for passivity toward things spiritual will move us toward that low-grade "joy in [our] works for a season" (3 Nephi 27:11). The combination of life and the light of Christ is designed to help us discern between the real thing and all the clever counterfeits and sparkling substitutes.

Moreover, there is no way to go around life. The only way to go is through. How, for instance, could the Lord teach us patience without the dimension of time and without also providing for us the relevant clinical experiences? How could we learn to place the cares and praise of the world in proper perspective without having encountered them? How else could we learn the differences between the holy and the profane? In what other way could we witness first-hand as between genuine gospel solutions and secular solutions? Some of the latter, though sincere, contain enormous errors, producing chickens which, when they come home to roost, will be full-grown pterodactyls!

Even with all the encompassing divine design, we can "make a mock of the great plan of redemption" (Jacob 6:8) by failing individually in this mortal school. Understandably, therefore, the prophets often speak in exhortational headlines, but also in loving summation: "O be wise; what can I say more?" (Jacob 6:12).

Submissiveness hastens the day when we shall see resplendent reality, things as they really were, really are, and really will become (Jacob 4:13; D&C 93:24).

The challenge, of course, is not only to become spiritually submissive to God but also to stay that way:

> For behold, the Spirit of the Lord hath already ceased to strive with their fathers; and they are without Christ and God in the world; and they are driven about as chaff before the wind.
>
> They were once a delightsome people, and they had Christ for their shepherd; yea, they were led even by God the Father.
>
> But now, behold, they are led about by Satan, even as chaff is driven before the wind, or as a vessel is tossed about upon the waves, without sail or anchor, or without anything wherewith to steer her; and even as she is, so are they (Mormon 5:16–18).

Mortality, this precious micro-dot on the canvas of eternity, is such a brief moment. While in it, we are to prepare ourselves for the time when there will be no time.

The strategic answers available to help us in this mortal moment are awesome. Where else but in the gospel of Jesus Christ in its restored fulness can one find the needed explanations for a God, perfect in His power and goodness, who nevertheless permits evil and suffering? Clearly, He desires to "set [us] up as a free people," if we will (3 Nephi 21:4). But will we then stay that way?

So often in life, it seems, a blessing is quickly succeeded by a stretching. Spiritual exhilaration is often short lived, being soon followed by vexation, temptation, and even tribulation. Perhaps this is so because we cannot handle exhilaration for any length of time. Or is it because we need to get on with the next challenge, there being so little time for languishing? Or is it that experiencing the sharp, side-by-side contrast of the sweet and the bitter, almost continuously, is essential until the very end of this mortal experience? Or are we at risk if in extended spiritual reveries we quickly forget others in need?

Whatever the reasons, the Lord hastens us forward—submissively on to the next work to be done. Handcarts are to be picked up again promptly, after pausing whether for gladness or for sadness. We are to "seek . . . first to *build up* the kingdom of God, and to *establish* His righteousness" (JST, Matthew 6:38, emphasis added). But we cannot build up the kingdom if we are tearing ourselves down. Thus we must deny ourselves certain things, including lust and immorality, as part of taking up the cross daily. Significantly, Jesus stresses this in His Nephite Sermon on the Mount (3 Nephi 12:27–30; Luke 9:23; JST, Luke 14:27). Temple covenants provide us with specific standards, and temple attendance with much-needed reminders of commitments made.

Submitting, but only episodically, is a telltale sign. Such reluctance is evidence of weak faith. So is putting off obedience. Sufficient submissiveness to kneel now means we will not be strangers to that posture later when "every knee shall bow and every tongue confess that Jesus is the Christ" (Romans 14:11; Philippians 2:10; D&C 76:110; 88:104). It will take no faith to renounce worldly things when these are among the ashes of a melted planet (3 Nephi 26:3; D&C 43:32; Ether 4:9).

Meanwhile, spiritual submissiveness brings about the wiser use of our time, talents, and gifts as compared with our laboring diligently but conditionally to establish our own righteousness instead of the Lord's (D&C 1:16). After all, Lucifer was willing to work very hard, but conditionally in his own way and for his own purposes (Moses 4:1).

Those who insist on walking in their own way will find that all such paths, however individualistic in appearance, will converge at that wide way and broad gate—where there will be a tremendous traffic jam.

Are we really ready, therefore, to accept the reality that there is only one Name and only one way whereby we can obtain salvation? (2 Nephi 31:21). Bending the knees of the intellect, then, requires us to:

> yield [ourselves] unto God, . . . as instruments of righteousness unto God (Romans 6:13).

> fast and pray oft, and [to] wax stronger and stronger in [our] humility, and firmer and firmer in the faith of Christ, unto the filling [our] souls with joy and consolation, yea, even to the purifying and the sanctification of [our] hearts, which sanctification cometh because of [our] yielding [our] hearts unto God (Helaman 3:35).

yield [ourselves] unto the Lord, and enter into his sanctuary (2 Chronicles 30:8).

Giving place in our souls and in our schedules, making room for God's words and work (Alma 32:27; see also 1 Nephi 21:20), requires intellectual submissiveness. It requires us to be responsive to all entreaties from the Lord, rather than being dependent upon thunderbolts to move us, or upon being commanded in all things (D&C 58:26–28). Submission requires sufficient dedication and perspiration to "try the experiment" of His gospel's goodness (Alma 34:4), to begin to follow Him in earnest.

When Jesus said, "Come, follow me," it was an invitation, not a taunt. Moreover, His firm footprints are especially recognizable. They reflect no hesitancy, and no turning aside; they lie in a straight path. The prints are also sunk inerasably deep into the soil of the second estate because of the heavy burdens He bore. A portion of that depth is attributable to us, individually, because we added to the heaviness of His pressing yoke.

Yet how can we have the necessary faith to be submissive if we are filled with sharp doubts and nagging questions?

2

"The Great Question"

Before we can submit to God and His plan, we must be persuaded to do so voluntarily. This requires that we have compelling and answering truths in response to life's key questions. So very much—whether attitudinal or behavioral—depends upon our living not by bread alone "but by every word that proceedeth out of the mouth of the Lord" (Deuteronomy 8:3; Matthew 4:4). And so much of the bread of life has been given to us.

Amulek designated "the great question" as whether there is really a redeeming Christ (Alma 34:5–6). The holy scriptures answer resoundingly and repetitively, "Yes! Yes! Yes!"

A loving Father-God has chosen to tell us much about the redeeming Christ and His "gospel" (3 Nephi 27:13–14, 21; D&C 33:12; 39:6; 76:40–41). This transcendent "good news" constitutes the resplendent, reassuring answers to the great question. The same affirmation comes with regard to all the related questions, such as those about human identity, the purpose and meaning of life, and whether we live beyond the grave.

God, who has created "worlds without number" (Moses 1:33, 37–38; see also Isaiah 45:18), reassures by revelation those of us on this tiny "speck of sand" who will heed His word and seek to do His will. We learn that "He doeth not anything save it be for the benefit of [this] world; for he loveth [this] world" (2 Nephi 26:24). "For behold," He has said, "this is my work and my glory—to bring to pass the immortality and eternal life of man" (Moses 1:39).

Central to that work is the ministry and the atonement of our Savior. In its recurring theme the Book of Mormon declares that "all things which have been given of God from the beginning of the world, unto man, are the typifying of [Christ]" (2 Nephi 11:4). And that means Christ in his submissive, self-negating role as the Savior and Redeemer.

The Apostle John wrote for the same reason, as did other prophets, "But these are written, that ye might believe that Jesus is the Christ, the Son of God; and that believing ye might have life through his name" (John 20:31).

It should not surprise us that this glorious gospel message is more perfect than any of its messengers, save Jesus only. Nor should it surprise us that the gospel message is more comprehensive than the comprehension of any of its bearers or hearers, save Jesus only.

Because the Restoration scriptures came forth in Bible Belt conditions early in this dispensation, we have been too slow to appreciate the special relevance of those scriptures to conditions in this the latter part of our dispensation. For instance, some scholars and even some clerics have developed questions and doubts about the historicity of Jesus. Such doubting and questioning was not pervasive in the America of the 1820s and 1830s. Demographically speaking, therefore, the greatest part of the impact of the Book of Mormon—with its convincing message that Jesus is the Christ—is occurring in our time, a time of deepening uncertainty and unrest. To answer affirmatively the great question is the very reason why the Book of Mormon and all Restoration scriptures were brought forth.

> And righteousness will I send down out of heaven; and truth will I send forth out of the earth, to bear testimony of mine Only Begotten; his resurrection from the dead; yea, and also the resurrection of all men; and righteousness and truth will I cause to sweep the earth as with a flood (Moses 7:62).

Fresh and additional witnesses of Jesus and the resurrection are especially needed in our unsubmissive age. The Book of Mormon is preeminently such a modern witness.

For those with ears to hear, the Book of Mormon also foretells the latter-day emergence of "other books" of witnessing scripture (1 Nephi 13:39–40), of which it is but one: "Proving to the world that the holy scriptures are true, and that God does inspire men and call them to his holy work in this age and generation, as well as in generations of old" (D&C 20:11).

The convergence of these "other books" of scripture with the precious Bible (whose essential truth they join in establishing) is part of the rhythm of the Restoration, providing us with an understanding of the God to whom we are to submit and of the laws and principles that make such submission appropriate and beneficial.

The presentation, translation, and publication of the Bible would have been impossible except for devoted and heroic individuals, including early Christian scholars and the Jewish prophets and others of antiquity. The "travails," "labors," and "pains" of these individuals preserved the Bible for us. Lamentably, as foreseen, as a people the Jews have been largely unthanked for that contribution. Instead they have often been "cursed," "hated," and made "game" of (2 Nephi 29:4–5; 3 Nephi 29:4, 8).

The existing scriptures make mention of more than twenty other books that will yet be restored (see 1 Nephi 19:10–16).[1] One day, in fact, "all things shall be revealed unto the children of men which ever have been . . . and which ever will be" (2 Nephi 27:11). Hence the ninth article of faith is such an impressive statement, full of promise for the obedient.

The "other books," particularly the Book of Mormon, fulfill Nephi's prophecy: "These last records . . . shall establish the truth of the first, which are of the twelve apostles of the Lamb" (1 Nephi 13:40). That is to say, what the latter-day seer, Joseph Smith, would bring forth would help many people in accepting God's word which had already gone forth, namely the Bible (2 Nephi 3:11), by convincing them "that the records of the prophets and of the twelve apostles of the Lamb are true" (1 Nephi 13:39). The Bible's role in mortal remembrance is crucial, and with that kind of remembrance can come needed obedience and submission to God's will.

> For behold, this is written for the intent that ye may believe that; and if ye believe that ye will believe this also; and if ye believe this ye will know concerning your

fathers, and also the marvelous works which were wrought by the power of God among them (Mormon 7:9).

The plenitude of the Restoration followed "a famine in the land, not a famine of bread, nor a thirst for water, but of hearing the words of the Lord" (Amos 8:11). The end of that famine was marked by the coming of the Book of Mormon and the "other books."

Such books of scripture have been and are the Lord's means of preserving the spiritual memory of centuries past, including the motivational examples of submissive spirits. Without such memory the generations slacken and die spiritually:

> There were many of the rising generation that . . . did not believe what had been said concerning the resurrection of the dead, neither did they believe concerning the coming of Christ (Mosiah 26:1–2).

> And at the time that Mosiah discovered them, . . . their language had become corrupted; and they had brought no records with them; and they denied the being of their Creator (Omni 1:17).

Belief in Deity and in the literal resurrection are usually the first beliefs to be discarded when faith diminishes. Ironically, though we gratefully accept the Bible as the word of God, the very process of its emergence—resulting in a dilution or loss of plain and precious truths—has, alas, led to a slackening or weakening of the Christian faith on the part of some—naturally, with an accompanying diminution of obedience to God's commandments. Because available Bible sources are not "originals," however, but represent dated derivations and translations, the "other books" of scripture which have come to us directly are even more to be prized.

Paul wrote his first epistle to the Corinthians about A.D. 56. We do not, of course, have that precious parchment. Instead, the earliest document involving the first epistle to the Corinthians is dated about A.D. 200. By comparison, King Benjamin's sermon (Mosiah chapters 2–5) was given in about 124 B.C. by a prophet under the tutelage of an angel. In the late fourth century A.D. this sermon was selected by another prophet—Mormon—for inclusion in the Book of Mormon. Benjamin's sermon was translated into English in A.D. 1829 by Joseph Smith, another prophet, through a process involving revelation. Thus there was an unbroken chain of a prophet-originator, a prophet-editor, and a prophet-translator in a remarkable process of collaborating witnesses.

For the serious reader, the Restoration scriptures provide a deeply significant response to modern man's architectonic needs—that is, our deep needs to discern some design, purpose, pattern, or plan regarding human existence.

No less than fifteen times, the Book of Mormon uses the word *plan* in connection with the plan of salvation or its components. Likewise the book of Moses signifies much in this summation: "And now, behold, I say unto you: This is the plan of salvation unto all men, through the blood of mine Only Begotten, who shall come in the meridian of time" (Moses 6:62).

The very use of the word *plan* in this connection is itself striking. In bringing back this particular "plain and precious" truth—that God not only lives but does have a loving and redeeming plan for mankind—the Book of Mormon is unusually relevant for our age and time. Phrases about God's planning for us from the creation or the "foundation of the world" appear not at all in the Old Testament, ten times in the New Testament, but thirty-five times in the "other books" (twenty-two times in the Book of Mormon, ten times in the Doctrine and Covenants, and three times in the Pearl of Great Price). *Foundation*, of course, denotes the creation, which was overseen by a loving and planning God.

Restoration scriptures lay further and heavy emphasis on the fact that the gospel has been with mankind from Adam on down. Only six pages into the Book of Mormon we read of the converging and testifying words of all the prophets "since the world began" (1 Nephi 3:20). Five pages later a recitation refers to the words of the "holy prophets from the beginning" (1 Nephi 5:13). The following single verse represents many:

> For behold, did not Moses prophesy unto them concerning the coming of the Messiah, and that God should redeem his people? Yea, and even all the prophets who have prophesied ever since the world began—have they not spoken more or less concerning these things? (Mosiah 13:33; see also 2 Nephi 25:19).

Other Restoration scriptures make similar declarations; for instance:

> And thus the Gospel began to be preached, from the beginning, being declared by holy angels sent forth

from the presence of God, and by his own voice, and by the gift of the Holy Ghost.

And thus all things were confirmed unto Adam, by an holy ordinance, and the Gospel preached, and a decree sent forth, that it should be in the world, until the end thereof; and thus it was. Amen (Moses 5:58–59).

If scholars in the future make any additional discoveries of ancient records pertaining to the Old and New Testaments, such may shrink the time between the origination of those scriptures and the earliest available documentation. However, any such *shrinking* will not lead to an automatic *enlarging* of faith. Future discoveries of inspired ancient documents may "throw greater views upon [the Savior's] gospel" (D&C 10:45), but these may also focus on portions of the gospel which existed *before* Jesus' mortal ministry. Unfortunately, some may then view such discoveries as diminishing the divinity of the Redeemer by implying that Jesus is, therefore, not Christianity's originator. For Latter-day Saints the dispensationalism of the Restoration and its doctrines of course removes any such concerns.

The restored gospel gives us a crystal-clear reading of the spiritual history of mankind, showing God's "tender mercies" (1 Nephi 1:20; Ether 6:12) from Adam on down. There is no need for us to be anxious about finding reliable portions of Christ's gospel extant before Christ's mortal ministry. After all, the gospel was preached and known from the beginning in the linkage with our first parents.

The linking together of the marvelous Restoration with

previous gospel dispensations was foreseen from the beginning and was foretold in the meridian of time: "Whom the heaven must receive until the times of restitution of all things, which God hath spoken by the mouth of all his holy prophets since the world began" (Acts 3:21).

Alma, after a discussion of the Fall, declared it was "expedient that man should know concerning the things whereof [God] had appointed unto them; therefore [God] sent angels to converse with them . . . and made known unto them the plan of redemption, which had been prepared from the foundation of the world" (Alma 12:28–30). This underscores dispensationalism but also discloses a process, the very revelatory process which was followed in the first half of the nineteenth century through angelic visitations to Joseph Smith.

At the center of the architectonic responsiveness of the Restoration scriptures is a steady, Christian core. It points not only to Jesus Christ but also to the submissive obedience of Saints throughout the ages. Jacob wrote: "We knew of Christ . . . many hundred years before his coming; . . . also all the holy prophets which were before us. Behold, they believed in Christ and worshipped the Father in his name . . . [keeping] the law of Moses, it pointing our souls to him" (Jacob 4:4–5). Jacob was emphatic: "None of the prophets have written . . . save they have spoken concerning this Christ" (Jacob 7:11). Moses and Abraham were part of this pattern:

> And now behold, Moses did not only testify of these things, but also all the holy prophets, from his days even to the days of Abraham.

Yea, and behold, Abraham saw of his coming, and was filled with gladness and did rejoice.

Yea, and behold I say unto you, that Abraham not only knew of these things, but there were many before the days of Abraham who were called by the order of God; yea, even after the order of his Son; and this that it should be shown unto the people, a great many thousand years before his coming, that even redemption should come unto them (Helaman 8:16–18).

For those of us who have eyes sufficiently submissive to see, God witnesses to us in so many ways besides through scripture. "Yea, and all things denote there is a God; yea, even the earth, and all things that are upon the face of it, yea, and its motion, yea, and also all the planets which move in their regular form do witness that there is a Supreme Creator" (Alma 30:44; see also Moses 6:63).

Therefore, as we come to know and accept the affirmative answers to the great question, we can, in Amulek's felicitous phrase, "live in thanksgiving daily" (Alma 34:38); that is, with a spirit and attitude that includes obedient gratitude for the many special conditions which make daily life on this earth possible.

Thankful remembrance, a submissive recognition of our dependence on the Lord, is an especially rich and repetitive theme in the Old Testament and the Book of Mormon:

Remember the days of old, consider the years of many generations: ask thy father, and he will shew thee; thy elders, and they will tell thee.

When the most High divided to the nations their

inheritance, when he separated the sons of Adam, he set the bounds of the people according to the number of the children of Israel.

For the Lord's portion is his people (Deuteronomy 32:7–9).

Then will I remember my covenant with Jacob, and also my covenant with Isaac, and also my covenant with Abraham will I remember; and I will remember the land. . . . I will . . . remember the covenant of their ancestors, whom I brought forth out of the land of Egypt in the sight of the heathen, that I might be their God (Leviticus 26:42, 45).

Behold, I would exhort you that when ye shall read these things . . . that ye would remember how merciful the Lord hath been unto the children of men, from the creation of Adam even down until the time that ye shall receive these things, and ponder it in your hearts (Moroni 10:3).

Our father, Lehi, also spake many things unto them, and rehearsed unto them, how great things the Lord had done for them in bringing them out of the land of Jerusalem (2 Nephi 1:1).

Every age needs the gospel's architectonic message and thankful remembrance, but none more desperately than our age, which is preoccupied with humanism, skepticism, and hedonism: "For how knoweth a man the master whom he has not served, and who is a stranger unto him, and is far from the thoughts and intents of his heart?" (Mosiah 5:13).

Even the title page[2] of the Book of Mormon declares, among other things, that the book was to advise posterity "what great things the Lord hath done for their fathers." The very lack of such a spiritual memory and of the appropriate spirit of thanksgiving once led to a decline of ancient Israel: "And also all that generation were gathered unto their fathers: and there arose another generation after them, which knew not the Lord, nor yet the works which he had done for Israel" (Judges 2:10).

Why was it so difficult for a whole people—or for Laman and Lemuel—to maintain faith? Because they were either uninformed or unbelieving as to "the dealings of that God who had created them" (1 Nephi 2:12; see also 2 Nephi 1:10). In the case of Laman and Lemuel many efforts were made: "I, Nephi, did teach my brethren these things; and . . . I did read many things to them, which were engraven upon the plates of brass, that they might know concerning the doings of the Lord in other lands, among people of old" (1 Nephi 19:22).

Granted, the great answers in the Restoration scriptures will not now be accepted by disbelievers. Such would not believe the Lord's words—whether coming through Paul or Joseph Smith—even if they had an original Pauline parchment or direct access to the gold plates. Referring principally to those plates, the Lord once comforted Joseph Smith by saying that such individuals would "not believe my words . . . if . . . [shown] all these things" (D&C 5:7).

Usually the "learned shall not read [these things], for they have rejected them" (2 Nephi 27:20). The reference suggests a mind-set of many of the learned of the world, who, by and large, if they know of it do not take the Book of Mormon seriously. Even when they read it, it is with a mind-set which excludes miracles, including the miracle of the book's coming forth by the "gift and power of God." Their flawed approach diverts them from scrutinizing the substance. Sometimes, as has been said, certain mortals are "so afraid of being taken in that they cannot be taken out"[3] of their mind-sets.

Obviously those with the anti-miracle mind-set discount the Book of Mormon because they cannot see the plates from which it was translated. Furthermore, some say, we do not know enough about the actual process of translation. But Moroni's inspired promise (Moroni 10:3–4) concerns reading and praying over the book's substance—not over the process of its production. That promise rests on a premise: The reader is (1) to read and ponder, (2) while remembering God's mercies to mankind from Adam until now, (3) to pray in the name of Christ, asking God with real intent if the book is true, (4) while exercising faith in Christ. If this premise is fulfilled, the promise is that God will manifest to the reader the truth of the book. The reverse approach, scanning while doubting, is the flipside of Moroni's methodology, and it produces flippant conclusions.

Jacob censured the "stiffnecked" Jews for "looking beyond the mark" (Jacob 4:14). We are looking beyond the mark today, for example, if we are more interested in the physical dimensions of the cross than in what Jesus achieved thereon; or when we neglect Alma's words on faith because we are too fascinated by the light-shielding hat reportedly used by Joseph Smith during some of the translating of the Book of Mormon.[4] To neglect substance while focusing on process is another form of unsubmissively looking beyond the mark.

Mankind, after all, is very dependent upon emancipating revelation: "Behold, great and marvelous are the works of the Lord. How unsearchable are the depths of the mysteries of him; and it is impossible that man should find out all his ways. And no man knoweth of his ways save it be revealed unto him; wherefore, brethren, despise not the revelations of God" (Jacob 4:8).

Clearly, we should not be deluded into thinking that these "other books" will be generally welcomed, particularly by those who say, "There cannot be any more" such books, and "we need no more" such books (2 Nephi 29:3, 6).

The Book of Mormon peoples, though Christians, were tied much more strictly to the pre-exilic Law of Moses until Jesus came than we in the Church have fully appreciated. "And, notwithstanding we believe in Christ, we keep the law of Moses, and look forward with steadfastness unto Christ, until the law shall be fulfilled" (2 Nephi 25:24). The Saints of those days were thus to "look forward unto the Messiah, and believe in him to come as though he already was" (Jarom 1:11). Moses indeed prophesied of the Messiah, but not all of his words are in the treasured Old Testament. Recall the walk of the resurrected Jesus with two disciples on the road to Emmaus. Their walk probably covered about twelve kilometers and provided ample time for Jesus' recitation of not merely the three or four now-surviving Old Testament verses but also many prophecies by Moses and others concerning Christ's mortal ministry (Luke 24:27).

The detailed correlation of all scripture in its testimony of Jesus Christ is marvelous to behold, especially as one considers the flow of Joseph Smith's pattern of translating. More than a hundred years before Christ's birth, King Benjamin prophe-sied: "And he shall be called Jesus Christ, the Son of God, the Father of heaven and earth, the Creator of all things from the beginning" (Mosiah 3:8). The resurrected Jesus introduced himself to the Nephites with strikingly similar words: "Behold, I am Jesus Christ the Son of God. I created the heav-ens and the earth, and all things that in them are. I was with the Father from the beginning" (3 Nephi 9:15).

Scriptures attesting to Jesus' divinity are vital in any age. Without their witness He will be considered a mere man (Mosiah 3:9) or "a thing of naught" (1 Nephi 19:9).

Over time there has occurred what has been called "the dilution of Christianity from within." This has resulted not only in a diminishing regard for Christ on the part of a number of theologians but also in their discounting the Resurrection, as Bultmann expressed it, as merely "a symbolic expression for the renewal of life for the disciples."[5] Once again, the supernal importance of the "other books" of scrip-ture is evident: they reinforce the reality of resurrection. Especially is this the effect of the Book of Mormon's addi-tional "gospel," 3 Nephi, with its report of the visitation of and instruction by the resurrected Jesus. The resurrection of many others also occurred and, by Jesus' pointed instruction, was written into the record, doubtless with our age in mind (see 3 Nephi 23:6–13).

In our day, many are not even asking the great question anymore; preoccupied, they regard Christianity "not as untrue or even as unthinkable, but simply irrelevant."[6] Some similar thinking existed in the times of the two Mosiahs (see Omni 1:17; Mosiah 28:1–2).

If the answer to the great question were no, then there would quickly come a wrenching surge of other questions. "If life has no meaning, why should I not please myself?" "Why should I deny myself anything?" "Why should I submit to any authority?"

Occasionally a member of the Church who is weak in the faith struggles with his other questions and circumstances and loses the battle. Those few members who desert the cause are abandoning an oasis to search for water in the desert. Some of them will not just wander off but will become obsessed critics occupying offices in the "great and spacious building" (1 Nephi 8:26–27; 11:35–36), that large but third-class hotel.

For believers, however, the great answers to the great question repeatedly focus us on the reality of the "great and last sacrifice," for "this is the whole meaning of the law, every whit pointing to that great and last sacrifice; and that great and last sacrifice will be the Son of God, yea, infinite and eternal" (Alma 34:14).

These great answers declare that mortal melancholy need not be, however frequently and poignantly it is expressed by those beset by it.

What we receive in the Restoration scriptures is solid and substantive. It is not a mere assemblage of aphorisms, nor is it simply the writings of a few individuals offering their philosophical opinions. It is rather the cumulative witness of prophetic individuals—each of them deeply committed to submission to God's will—especially those who were eyewitnesses of Jesus, including Lehi, Nephi, Jacob, Alma, the brother of Jared, Mormon, Moroni, and Joseph Smith. The biblical account that five hundred brothers and sisters

witnessed the resurrected Jesus (1 Corinthians 15:6) is joined
by the witnessing throng of 2,500 in the land of Bountiful
(3 Nephi 17:25). All of these add to the burgeoning cloud of
witnesses about whom the Apostle Paul wrote (Hebrews
12:1).

Instead of witnessing for Christ, the Book of Mormon
might have been another kind of book. It could have been
chiefly concerned with the ebb and flow of governmental history; i.e., "Princes come and princes go, an hour of pomp, an
hour of show." We have many such books already, each remi-
niscent in one way or another of the hopelessness reflected in
these lines from Shelley:

> . . . Two vast and trunkless legs of stone
> Stand in the desert. Near them, on the sand,
> Half sunk, a shattered visage lies, . . .
> And on the pedestal, these words appear—
> "My name is Ozymandias, King of Kings:
> Look on my works, ye Mighty, and despair!"
> Nothing beside remains. Round the decay
> Of that colossal wreck, boundless and bare,
> The lone and level sands stretch far away.[7]

Because the editing of the Book of Mormon, with its witnessing gospel of hope, occurred under divine direction, it has
a focus which is essentially spiritual. Yet some still criticize the
book for not being what it was never intended to be, as if one
could justifiably criticize a phone directory for lack of a plot.

Even so, not all verses of scripture are of equal significance. For instance, some verses in the Book of Mormon are
of tremendous salvational significance, others less so. The

book of Ether has a verse about lineage history: "And Jared had four sons," and so on (Ether 6:14). However, Ether also contains another verse of tremendous salvational significance:

> And if men come unto me I will show unto them their weakness. I give unto men weakness that they may be humble; and my grace is sufficient for all men that humble themselves before me; for if they humble themselves before me, and have faith in me, then will I make weak things become strong unto them (Ether 12:27).

We read of a battle " . . . when . . . they slept upon their swords . . . were drunken with anger, even as a man who is drunken with wine; . . . and when the night came there were thirty and two of the people of Shiz, and twenty and seven of the people of Coriantumr" (Ether 15:20–25). Such numerical accounting, however, is of a much lower spiritual significance for the development of accountable discipleship than are these lines, the most complete delineation of Jesus' requirement that we become as little children (see Matthew 18:3):

> . . . and becometh as a child, submissive, meek, humble, patient, full of love, willing to submit to all things which the Lord seeth fit to inflict upon him, even as a child doth submit to his father (Mosiah 3:19).

One reason to "search the scriptures" is to discover these luxuriant meadows of meaning, these green pastures that can nourish us in our individual times of need. The Book of Mormon surely has its share of these. Immediately after words about economic conditions in the now-vanished city of Helam, we encounter an enduring and bracing truth:

"Nevertheless the Lord seeth fit to chasten his people; yea, he trieth their patience and their faith" (Mosiah 23:20–21; see also D&C 98:12; Abraham 3:25).

Similarly, the Book of Mormon provides us with insights we may not yet be ready to manage fully. Astonishingly, Alma includes our pains, sicknesses, and infirmities, along with our sins, among that which Jesus would also "take upon him" (Alma 7:11–12). The Atonement included the perfecting of Christ's mercy by His experiencing "according to the flesh." Nephi in exclaiming, "O how great the plan of our God!" (2 Nephi 9:13) also declared that Jesus would suffer "the pains of all . . . men, women, and children, who belong to the family of Adam" (2 Nephi 9:21). The soul trembles at the implications of these statements. One comes away from such verses weeping, deepened in his adoration of our Redeemer.

When we "search the scriptures," the luminosity of various verses in the various books is focused. This illumination arcs and then converges, even though we are dealing with different authors, people, places, and times: "Wherefore, I speak the same words unto one nation like unto another. And when the two nations shall run together the testimony of the two nations shall run together also" (2 Nephi 29:8).

But believing is not a matter of accessing antiquity to obtain its evidence, though we welcome such evidence. Nor is it solely dependent upon accumulating welcome historical evidence. Rather it is a matter of believing in "Jesus' words." Real faith, like real humility, is developed "because of the word," and not because of surrounding circumstances (Alma 32:13–14).

How fitting it is that it should be so! The test is focused on the message, not on the messengers. On principles, not on process. On doctrines, not on plot. The emphasis is on belief *per se*, "because of the word." As Jesus told Thomas, on the eastern hemisphere, "Blessed are they that have not seen, and yet have believed" (John 20:29). He proclaimed to the Nephites, "More blessed are they who shall believe in your words because that ye shall testify that ye have seen me" (3 Nephi 12:2).

True faith is not to be brought about by overwhelming and intimidating intervention from God, either. The Lord is a shepherd with a "mild" and "pleasant" voice—not a shouting and scolding sheepherder (Helaman 5:30–31; 3 Nephi 11:3). Those who demand a "voiceprint" of the "voice of the Lord" probably would not like His doctrines anyway (see John 6:66). The things of the Spirit are to be "sought by faith"; they are not to be seen through slit-eyed skepticism.

Without real faith and its attendant submissiveness, people sooner or later find one thing or another to stumble over (Romans 9:32). After all, it is very difficult to show to the provincial and proud things which they "never had supposed" (Moses 1:10), or things they do not really want to know. When Jesus was speaking about himself as the bread of life, a powerful doctrine laden with behavior-changing implications, there was murmuring in the audience. Jesus asked them, "Doth this offend you?" (John 6:61). "Blessed is he, whosoever shall not be offended in me" (Luke 7:23).

Given all the foregoing, it is touching that a jailed Joseph Smith, during his last mortal night—June 26, 1844—bore "a powerful testimony to the guards of the divine authenticity of the Book of Mormon, the restoration of the gospel, the administration of angels"[8] (see Alma 12:28–30). The guards apparently did not hearken then any more than most of the world hearkens now. But heeded or unheeded, the Book of Mormon has a further rendezvous to keep:

> Wherefore, these things shall go from generation to generation as long as the earth shall stand; and they shall go according to the will and pleasure of God; and the nations who shall possess them shall be judged of them according to the words which are written (2 Nephi 25:22).

Thus the Book of Mormon will be with us "as long as the earth shall stand." We need all that time to explore it, for the book is like a vast mansion with gardens, towers, courtyards, and wings. There are rooms yet to be entered, with flaming fireplaces waiting to warm us. The rooms glimpsed so far contain further furnishings and rich detail yet to be savored, but decor dating from Eden is evident. There are panels inlaid with incredible insights, particularly insights about the great question. Yet we as Church members sometimes behave like hurried tourists, scarcely venturing beyond the entry hall.

The mansion represents the divine order to be expected in "a marvelous work and a wonder"—all this in an age when so many things have been turned "upside down" (Isaiah 29:14, 16). Only an abundant restitution could begin to set things right, and one of the first things to be set right would be man's relationship with God—an obedience as to our divine Father.

3

"A Marvellous Work"

The Restoration brought a flood of faith-building truths that would develop a Zion people, a covenant people, a people willing to obey God's commandments and submit to His will. Isaiah described the Restoration as a "*marvellous work and a wonder*" (Isaiah 29:14; emphasis added). The Hebrew roots for "wonder" refer to things "beyond human capability," the "miraculous."

An angel told Nephi that God would one day perform "a great and a marvelous work among the children of men" (1 Nephi 14:7; see also 2 Nephi 25:17; 27:26; 3 Nephi 21:9; 28:32). In 1829 the Lord, who planned the schedule of the Restoration, including the coming forth of the Book of Mormon, announced: "Now behold, a marvelous work is about to come forth among the children of men" (D&C 4:1).

Following the centuries-long famine foreseen by Amos (Amos 8:11–12), with the deepening of doubts in its wake, the Restoration finally came. As Church members we have not even completed our full inventory of the harvest.

In terms of our capacity to comprehend, the Restoration

is like the Malachi measure: "there shall not be room enough to receive it" (Malachi 3:10). Not only have "other books" of abundant scripture come forth, as already mentioned, but more will. The additional scriptures have come forth in a time when, sadly, the Bible is less and less read in the world; it is ignored by most and even impugned by some. As a result, "an exceedingly great number do stumble" (1 Nephi 13:29), giving rise to decreased faith in and obedience to God. Hence the relevance of the Restoration.

Just as was foreseen, the scriptures of the Restoration, fusing and growing together with the Bible, have resulted in a "confounding of false doctrines" (2 Nephi 3:12) and "the taking away of . . . stumbling blocks" (1 Nephi 14:1). The Restoration scriptures, among other blessings, answer the questions that have tormented ecclesiastical councils and synods in centuries past.

While Church members rejoice in the richness, relevance, and remarkability of the Restoration, given its miraculous dimensions we should not be surprised when the Church is challenged or when the divinity behind the Restoration is questioned. The smug, like those of Christ's day who despised anything coming out of Nazareth, simply ignore the Restoration. Some dare not hope, for fear of being disappointed. Some are comfortably adjusted to the carnal and want no reminding interference from the spiritual. Thus the reactions to the Restoration cross a spectrum from rage to rejoicing. Little wonder that it is so, because the Restoration so profoundly affects our views of God, self, others, life, and even the universe. Given the pervasive secularization of society, the Restoration came none too soon.

To illustrate the illumination which flows from the Restoration, we will note some comparisons.

Though we are grateful for all scripture, including the Holy Bible, the Restoration often replaces comparative scarcity with rich abundance by bringing back "plain and precious truths" (1 Nephi 13:39–40). For instance, concerning the foundational truths—such as the determining premortal council in heaven, the Fall, and this life as a probationary period—an abundant two or three times more divine data are given through the Restoration than was previously available. Moreover, the gains are not only in quantity but also in clarity.

As examples, Job's curtain-parting "sons of God shouting for joy" in the Bible (Job 38:7) is helpful. So is the verse indicating Jeremiah's foreordination (Jeremiah 1:5). But these glimpses of the reality of premortality now company with stunning Restoration verses about foreordination and divine purpose, as in the third chapter of Abraham, wherein glimpses become vistas:

> Now the Lord had shown unto me, Abraham, the intelligences that were organized before the world was; and among all these there were many of the noble and great ones;
>
> And God saw these souls that they were good, and he stood in the midst of them, and he said: These I will make my rulers; for he stood among those that were spirits, and he saw that they were good; and he said unto me: Abraham, thou art one of them; thou wast chosen before thou wast born (Abraham 3:22–23; see also D&C 138:53).

This holy order of leadership is discussed as well by Alma and by Nephi the son of Helaman:

> Yea, and behold I say unto you, that Abraham not only knew of these things, but there were many before the days of Abraham who were called by the order of God; yea, even after the order of his Son; and this that it should be shown unto the people, a great many thousand years before his coming, that even redemption should come unto them (Helaman 8:18; see also Alma 13:2–5).

The scope of God's encompassing divine design is also enlarged dramatically by the doctrine of the plurality of worlds. Speaking of Jesus, John tells us that "all things were made by him" (John 1:3), and Paul makes similar expressions in "by whom also he made the worlds" and "the worlds were framed by the word of God" (Hebrews 1:2; 11:3). In addition we learn: "And worlds without number have I created; and I also created them for mine own purpose; and by the Son I created them, which is mine Only Begotten" (Moses 1:33; see also 1:39). How could one not be willing to submit his life to such a transcendent intelligence and purpose?

As a result, the believing disciple does not view the cosmos as "godless geometric space." Instead, when he observes the earth, the sun, the moon, and the stars, he senses that "any man who hath seen any or the least of these hath seen God moving in his majesty and power" (D&C 88:47). Of these worlds we learn further that "the inhabitants thereof are begotten sons and daughters unto God" (D&C 76:24). It is all more than we can really comprehend.

The Restoration has added abundance to Isaiah's words about divine purposes for this earth: "[God] created it not in vain, he formed it to be inhabited" (Isaiah 45:18; see also 1 Nephi 17:36). We have the words of the Lord that His work and glory is "to bring to pass the immortality and eternal life of man" (Moses 1:39). This purposeful planet is, in fact, a proving and testing school.

> And we will prove them herewith, to see if they will do all things whatsoever the Lord their God shall command them (Abraham 3:25).

> Nevertheless the Lord seeth fit to chasten his people; yea, he trieth their patience and their faith (Mosiah 23:21).

> For he will give unto the faithful line upon line, precept upon precept; and I will try you and prove you herewith (D&C 98:12).

In still other situations, the Restoration provides clarification. As prophesied, the rising sun of the Restoration melts away the icy stumbling blocks of false doctrines frozen in place over the centuries (1 Nephi 14:1). Several examples follow.

Predestination, once so powerful an influence on the human scene (and not without its residual presence today), is overturned by the doctrines of premortal existence and of foreordination. Instead of an arbitrary, unmerited "chosenness," the merits of individuals meet the beckoning call of God. "And this is the manner after which they were ordained—being called and prepared from the foundation of the world according to the foreknowledge of God, on account of their exceeding faith and good works" (Alma 13:3; see also Jeremiah 1:5; Alma 13:3–5; Abraham 3:23; D&C 138:53–55).

Predestination's capriciousness provided an excuse for some to disbelieve in any God at all. Its falsity—like that of other incorrect doctrines—gave unsubmissiveness a false legitimacy.

Ex nihilo creation—viewing mortals as having been created out of nothing—with all of its attendant problems that include blurred accountability, is refuted by Restoration light. We know now that not only was Jesus in the beginning with the Father (D&C 93:21), but we were also (D&C 93:23)! Clear truths about the relationship of the Father and the Son came not only in the theophany of 1820 but also in revelations so richly given to Joseph Smith, such as this one in 1833:

> And I, John, saw that [Christ] received not of the fulness at the first, but received grace for grace;
>
> And he received not of the fulness at first, but continued from grace to grace, until he received a fulness;
>
> And thus he was called the Son of God, because he received not of the fulness at the first (D&C 93:12–14).

We need such truths lest, as with the woman of Samaria (John 4:19–22), we know not whom we worship. "I give unto you these sayings that you may understand and know how to worship, and know what you worship, that you may come unto the Father in my name, and in due time receive of his fulness" (D&C 93:19; see also verses 1–18).

Furthermore, as to mankind's "origins" we have this mind-expanding Restoration statement: "Man was also in the beginning with God. Intelligence, or the light of truth, was not created or made, neither indeed can be" (D&C 93:29).

Someday we will be able to see causality more clearly, including how the false doctrine of an *ex nihilo* creation has caused confusion about human identity and the human condition. Admittedly we do not now understand all the implications of the words, "spirits . . . have no beginning; they existed before . . . for they are . . . eternal" (Abraham 3:18). Yet we surely understand enough to see a loving and redeeming God at work, striving to help us become as He is—a cause for our deep gratitude and joy, instead of despair and doubt, and for a willing submission to whatever He perceives will further that purpose.

After centuries of official silence, the doctrines pertaining to the potential exaltation of man are likewise given in Restoration scripture. *Apotheosis* has been restored sufficiently to inform us as to our true identities and possibilities. Otherwise, if Jesus and we were not of the same order as God the Father, could we really do as Jesus commanded and strive to become "even as" the Father? (Matthew 5:48; 3 Nephi 12:48; 27:27.)

The doleful effects of misunderstanding about Adam's transgression, the so-called *original sin*, are dispelled by the Restoration. The second article of faith declares: "We believe that men will be punished for their own sins, and not for Adam's transgression." Further, "Every spirit of man was innocent in the beginning; and God having redeemed man

from the fall, men became again, in their infant state, innocent before God" (D&C 93:38).

Indeed, "the Son of God hath atoned for original guilt,
wherein the sins of the parents cannot be answered upon the
heads of the children, for they are whole from the foundation
of the world" (Moses 6:54). Though born into a sinful and
imperfect world to experience death, each of us can so live as
to ensure that the spiritual in us triumphs over the carnal; if
we will follow the Savior's pattern of submission to the
Father's will, we can have joy in this life and a fulness of joy
in the world to come.

Imbedded in the profound truths of the Restoration is
relief from the painful dilemmas which have caused some to
stumble and fall. Significant answers are now available to cruel
questions such as "If God is good and omnipotent, why does
He permit suffering and evil?" In response thereto we learn
important truths about the combined consequences of *misused agency* and about the role of *divine tutoring*. Some *challenges* built into life are *"common to all men." Infant mortality*
is not left as a dangling dilemma. And in the just plan of God
there are provisions for *those who do not hear the gospel in mortality.* These and other answers underscore the *ultimate justice
and mercy* of God.

We can rely on the mercy of a loving God, for we are at
the center of His redemptive work. Our God is surely no
stranger to the successful, continuing execution of His plan of
salvation, the plan of happiness. How it helps our faith, and
further justifies our obedience to His wishes, to know a little
about God's larger design!

As indicated above, individual moral agency is now

better understood, for we live in the context of *a choosing mankind* and *a proving God.*

> Wherefore, men are free according to the flesh; . . . And they are free to choose liberty and eternal life, through the great Mediator of all men, or to choose captivity and death, according to the captivity and power of the devil; for he seeketh that all men might be miserable like unto himself (2 Nephi 2:27; see also Abraham 3:25).

Restoration scriptures inform us of still other soul-stretchings, unrelated to wrong choices. Some occur because the Lord, desiring our submissiveness, tutors us (Mosiah 3:19; 23:21). As Joseph Smith heard in Liberty Jail, "all these things shall give thee experience, and shall be for thy good" (D&C 122:7). Yes, "men are that they might have joy"; "nevertheless, thou mayest choose for thyself" (Moses 3:17). In the midst of "all these things," Jesus our Exemplar is the Perfect Shepherd. We can safely cast our cares upon a completely empathic Savior (1 Peter 5:7).

From the beginning an informing and loving God has "made known unto [mankind] the plan of redemption," but he has done so in a metered way, "according to their faith and repentance and their holy works" (Alma 12:28–30).

Though we cannot fully fathom the matter now, at judgment time all of us will, in Alma's words, "acknowledge . . . that all [God's] judgments are just . . . and that he is merciful unto the children of men" (Alma 12:15). Then, as Abinadi expressed it, "people shall see eye to eye and shall confess before God that his judgments are just" (Mosiah 16:1). The mortal Messiah came to experience "all these things"; He thus gained a knowledge of things "according to the flesh" and was thereby perfected in His empathy by the Atonement, understanding personally not only pain born of sins but also the pains, grief, and sicknesses through which we pass. Under the direction of the Father, Christ will thus be able to render perfect justice, and we will know it and will acknowledge it (Alma 7:11–12; 2 Nephi 9:21).

In a unique manner the Restoration responds in special, second-mile ways to the concerns of those who may sincerely seek further assurances about the divinity of Jesus. Through the Restoration's richness the Holy Bible's witness about the divinity of Jesus is, in fact, established: "For behold, this [the Book of Mormon] is written for the intent that ye may believe that [the Bible]" (Mormon 7:9; see also 1 Nephi 13:39–40).

What the Restoration brings clearly into our view discloses a many-splendored Savior, not simply a Socrates in Samaria or a Plato in Palestine.

Some worry that there is very little in secular history about Jesus, with only some minor mention in the writings of Tacitus, Suetonius, and Josephus.[1] We grant the imperfections of all secular history and the paucity of its references to Jesus. Instead of recommending secular history, however, Jesus told us to search the scriptures, for it is they which testify of Him (John 5:39). Thus we see the great importance of the additional "other books" of scripture serving as further testaments of Jesus' reality and divinity.

Some fret because the four New Testament Gospels are imperfect historical documents, having been written years after Jesus' crucifixion. Yet the precious biblical record is essentially true. There are some translation limitations (see Articles of Faith 1:8). Certain transmission limitations are more serious, however (see 1 Nephi 13:34, 39–40). "And now, Moses, my son, I will speak unto thee concerning this earth upon which thou standest, and thou shalt write the things which I shall speak. And in a day when the children of men shall esteem my words as naught and take many of them from the book which thou shalt write, behold, I will raise up another like unto thee; and they shall be had again among the children of men—among as many as shall believe" (Moses 1:40–41).

Nevertheless, the "other books" clearly establish the essential truths of the Bible, and the book of 3 Nephi joins the New Testament as another testament of Jesus.

Some fear that the Gospel of John may not actually have been written by him. The Restoration makes it clear, however, that John was actually assigned by the Lord to write certain scripture, whether the book of Revelation, or his Gospel, or those and other writings as well. "But the things which thou shalt see hereafter thou shalt not write; for the Lord God hath ordained the apostle of the Lamb of God that he should write them" (1 Nephi 14:25).

What John wrote was "plain and pure, and most precious and easy to the understanding of all men" (1 Nephi 14:23; see also 20–27; D&C 88:141). Multiple and validating references to John's writings are in the "other books" of scripture. However, the fulness of John's record is yet to be revealed. "And then shall my revelations which I have caused to be written by my servant John be unfolded in the eyes of all the people" (Ether 4:16).

It is likewise so with another John, John the Baptist: "And John saw and bore record of the fulness of my glory, and the fulness of John's record is hereafter to be revealed" (D&C 93:6).

Verses in John the Revelator's writings have actually been catalytic in bringing forth Restoration scripture. John 5:29 brought forth Doctrine and Covenants 76. John 21:20–23 brought forth Doctrine and Covenants 7.

Furthermore, Peter, James, and John ordained Joseph Smith to the Melchizedek Priesthood, and gave him the apostleship and certain keys of the last dispensation (see D&C 27:12; 35:18–20). Thus John has been seen, more of his words have been given to us, and more are yet to come.

Some scholars lament that the New Testament contains no actual eyewitness accounts of the Resurrection, because its sources are not originals. But the Restoration's evidences are emphatic, including that of the "fifth gospel." Having sufficient records does matter. "Now it came to pass that there were many of the rising generation that . . . did not believe the tradition of their fathers. They did not believe what had been said concerning the resurrection of the dead, neither did they believe concerning the coming of Christ" (Mosiah 26:1–2; see also Omni 1:17).

Without such records and sufficient familiarity with them, belief in Jesus and the Resurrection are often discarded (see Judges 2:10–13). With such rejection, there can be no submission.

As to more eyewitnesses of the resurrected Jesus, 2,500 so testified (3 Nephi 11:13–17; 16:4; 17:25). The resurrected Jesus gave a pointed reminder to the Nephites to record that the graves of many resurrected Saints opened; He wanted the record as to the resurrection to be clear (3 Nephi 23:7–13; Matthew 27:52). Thus many eyewitnesses on both hemispheres affirm the reality of the resurrection of Jesus and of many others as well.

A few scholars also question, or at least ponder, whether Jesus really claimed to be the Messiah, and whether His followers so understood. Or was Jesus just another charismatic moralist or minor prophet?

The New Testament is *clear*: John 4:25–26; 6:69; 20:31. The Book of Mormon is *emphatic*: Mosiah 3:5–10; 3 Nephi, chapters 9 through 11.

Furthermore, Jesus is Lord of not just one of them but all the prophets. He has been interactive with all prophets—Old Testament and New Testament alike. He visited Adam and his righteous posterity in Adam-ondi-Ahman three years before Adam's death (D&C 107:53–55).

According to Joseph Smith, on a high mountain Moses received the endowment.[2] Peter, James, and John with Jesus, Moses, and Elias on the Mount of Transfiguration received priesthood keys, and, according to another modern prophet, Joseph Fielding Smith, perhaps the endowment.[3] In the Kirtland Temple, Jesus, Moses, and Elias blessed Joseph Smith and conferred upon him keys much needed for the rolling forward of God's work in the last dispensation.

Thus Jesus is Lord of all the prophets, and He continues to call and to prepare them. Part of that preparation involves their submission to His will. Could we imagine the Restoration taking place without a compliant Joseph Smith? Indeed, we have long recognized that God sometimes calls young men to be prophets (Samuel, Nephi, for example) because their ways are not set in worldly traditions.

The New Testament is *clear* as to the special relationship of Jesus to the Father. The Restoration scriptures are even more so. Jesus in the great intercessory prayer pleaded, "And now, O Father, glorify thou me with thine own self with the glory which I had with thee before the world was" (John 17:5; see also John 5:19; 8:28).

The Restoration's temples, scriptures, and revelations are *emphatic* regarding Jesus' special relationship with the Father (see Moses 1:33; D&C 19:17–19; 76:24; 88:47). Jesus is the Father's *firstborn* spirit son and the *Only Begotten* Son in the flesh. He has a special relationship with the Father, indeed!

The "Abba experience" in Gethsemane also affirms that Jesus had a special relationship with God. The suffering Jesus there addressed God as "Abba," meaning "Father, dear," a most familiar form of address that was fully justified by Jesus' unique relationship with the Father. In the extremity of his suffering, Jesus beseeched the Father to take the cup from Him "if it be possible" (Matthew 26:39). The agony—though anticipated by Him from premortal times—apparently was so much worse than even Jesus had imagined; He was, as prophesied, "very heavy" (Mark 14:33; Psalm 69:20–21). "Nevertheless," said the ever-submissive Savior, "not as I will, but as thou wilt" (Matthew 26:39).

Luke's report about Jesus' sweating "as it were great drops of blood falling down to the ground" (Luke 22:44) is fully validated and is elaborated upon as well in the "other books" of scripture: "Which suffering caused myself, even God, the greatest of all, to bleed at every pore, and to suffer both body

and spirit—and would that I might not drink the bitter cup, and shrink" (D&C 19:18).

The shedding of Jesus' blood thus was accomplished not only in the scourging and on Calvary but also earlier in Gethsemane. A recent and thoughtful article by several physicians on the physical death of Jesus Christ indicates that "the severe scourging with its intense pain and appreciable blood loss, most probably left Jesus in a preshock state" (we recall that He needed help to carry the cross), "therefore, even before the actual crucifixion, Jesus' physical condition was at least serious, and possibly critical. . . . Although scourging may have resulted in considerable blood loss, crucifixion per se was a relatively bloodless procedure."[4]

How wondrous and marvelous that the Savior would endure all that the Atonement involved—and for us! How helpful in building our faith in Christ, so that with His perfect example of submission we can be more adequately obedient!

For those who truly desire to live not by bread alone, but by every word which proceeds forth from the Lord, there will be no famine. In fact, the harvest of the Restoration is "running over."

4

"The Infinite Atonement"

Christ's atonement is the centerpiece of human history. The Restoration scriptures both confirm the fact and amplify the information concerning this crucial reality.

Both Jacob and Amulek declared it to be an "infinite atonement" (2 Nephi 9:7; Alma 34:8–12). First, the sacrifice of an imperfect and finite human would not have satisfied the requirements of divine justice. A mere mortal could not have performed the Atonement. Divine justice thus required that, if the repentant were not to have to pay for their own sins, the Only Begotten of the Father should lay down His life voluntarily for that purpose:

> No man taketh it from me, but I lay it down of myself. I have power to lay it down, and I have power to take it again. This commandment have I received of my Father (John 10:18).

> For it is expedient that there should be a great and last sacrifice; yea, not a sacrifice of man, neither of beast, neither of any manner of fowl; for it shall not be a

human sacrifice; but it must be an infinite and eternal sacrifice.

Now there is not any man that can sacrifice his own blood which will atone for the sins of another (Alma 34:10–11).

Why so great a sacrifice? Because all of us mortals need it, along with time and space—room to repent and grow, so that one day, if submissive, we can be worthy to return to the presence of God:

> For behold, if Adam had put forth his hand immediately, and partaken of the tree of life, he would have lived forever, according to the word of God, having *no space for repentance*; yea, and also the word of God would have been void, and the great plan of salvation would have been frustrated (Alma 42:5, emphasis added).

Furthermore, only in an "infinite atonement" would mercy overpower the stern demands of justice (see Alma 34:15). The mercy of God responds to our helpless condition: "Since man had fallen he could not merit anything of himself; but the sufferings and death of Christ atone for their sins, through faith and repentance" (Alma 22:14).

Second, the infinite atonement is fully comprehensive in the immortalizing benefits it provides to all of God's children by the grace of God (see Alma 11:40–44). "The atonement which is infinite for all mankind" (2 Nephi 25:16) provides infinite benefits "according to the great plan of the Eternal God" who foresaw the Fall and who mercifully decreed "there must be an atonement made" (Alma 34:9).

A third dimension may be seen in the infinite intensiveness of Christ's suffering. This intensiveness required a fully atoning and fully comprehending Atoner who would "know according to the flesh" human pain, sorrow, grief, and misery (Alma 7:11–12). "For behold, he suffereth the pains of all men, yea, the pains of every living creature, both men, women, and children, who belong to the family of Adam" (2 Nephi 9:21).

Thus, in addition to bearing our sins—the required essence of the Atonement—the "how" of which we surely do not understand, Jesus is further described as having come to know our sicknesses, griefs, pains, and infirmities as well. Another "how" we cannot now comprehend (see Isaiah 53:4; Matthew 8:17; Mosiah 14:4; Alma 7:11–12)! Jesus thus not only satisfied the requirements of divine justice but also, particularly in His Gethsemane and Calvary ordeals, demonstrated and perfected His capacity to succor His people and his empathy for them. He came to know, personally and perfectly, "according to the flesh," how to help us become more like His fully comprehending Father: "Great is our Lord, and of great power: his understanding is infinite" (Psalm 147:5).

Jesus' daily mortal experiences and His ministry, to be sure, acquainted Him by observation with a sample of human sicknesses, grief, pains, sorrows, and infirmities which are "common to man" (1 Corinthians 10:13). But the agonies of the Atonement were infinite and first-hand! Since not all human sorrow and pain is connected to sin, the full intensiveness of the Atonement involved bearing our pains, infirmities, and sicknesses, as well as our sins. Whatever our sufferings, we can safely cast our "care upon him; for he careth for [us]" (1 Peter 5:7).

Jesus is a fully comprehending Christ.

The Atonement, then, was infinite in the *divineness* of the one sacrificed, in the *comprehensiveness* of its coverage, and in the *intensiveness*—incomprehensible to us—of the Savior's suffering.

Additionally, since Jesus is the creator of other worlds whose inhabitants are also "begotten sons and daughters unto God" (D&C 76:24), it may be that the benefits of the Atonement will extend to all of the spirit children of our Father in Heaven, wherever situated.[1] Obviously, since "as in Adam all die, even so in Christ shall all be made alive" (1 Corinthians 15:22), the benefits of Jesus' atonement passed to more than those of the Jerusalem fold at the site of the drama. In fact, the Redeemer declared to those at Jerusalem that He had other sheep (John 10:16). Later, to the Nephite fold, Jesus announced that He had still other sheep (3 Nephi 15:21; 16:1). How many folds there are we know not.

Therefore, unto this parable I will liken all these kingdoms, and the inhabitants thereof—every kingdom in its hour, and in its time, and in its season, even according to the decree which God hath made (D&C 88:61).

Of this particular verse, President John Taylor said, "That is, each kingdom, or planet, and the inhabitants thereof, were blessed with the visits and presence of their Creator, in their several times and seasons."[2]

Concerning this expansiveness, Elder Marion G. Romney observed:

> John's testimony is conclusive that Jesus is the Lord of the universe as well as the Lord of this earth: "I saw his glory, that he was in the beginning, *before the world was*; . . . The *worlds* were made by him; *men were made* by him; *all things* were made *by him*, and through him, and of him"[3] (D&C 93:7, 10).

Thus the Atonement *may* reach into the universe—even as its blessings and redemptive powers reach into the small universe of each individual's suffering. How infinite, indeed!

No wonder the suffering of such an infinite atonement would produce blood at every pore (see D&C 19:18)!

To the repentant, battered, bruised, and alienated the Deliverer's promise is deliverable: "I shall heal them" (3 Nephi 18:32). He knows, perfectly and personally, how to succor each of us in our infirmities, if only we are "willing to submit" (Alma 7:11–12).

The Book of Mormon contains literally dozens of references to the Atonement, referring to it, for instance, as "the great and last sacrifice" (Alma 34:13–14). It is also a sacrifice which is described as being "infinite and eternal" (Alma 34:10). In the Atonement is found the "whole meaning of the law" of Moses (Alma 34:14). It is by means of the Atonement that the "resurrection [will] pass upon all men" (2 Nephi 9:22). Though mercy "overpowereth justice," justice is still fully satisfied by virtue of infinite suffering (Alma 34:15; 42:24–25).

Given what are to us the incomprehensible agonies and

transcendent consequences of Gethsemane, no wonder King Benjamin declared that Christ would suffer "even more than man can suffer, except it be unto death; for behold, blood cometh from every pore, so great shall be his anguish" (Mosiah 3:7). That blood in each and every pore further symbolizes infiniteness.

Knowing as we do that before the scourging and crucifixion Jesus bled at every pore in Gethsemane, how red His raiment must have been then, how crimson His cloak!

No wonder that, in one of His appearances—when He comes in power and glory—Christ will come in red attire (D&C 133:48), thereby not only signifying the winepress of wrath but also bringing to our remembrance how He suffered, for each of us, in Gethsemane and on Calvary!

There are so many subduing reasons to submit and surrender to Him and to our Father's purposes—not out of intimidation, but out of deep appreciation. Jesus was infinitely obedient, suffering an infinite number of things, yet He made possible eternal life with its promise of eternal increase for the elect. This is another dimension of the ongoing, infinite atonement's benefits.

Repeatedly God has described His course as reiterative, "one eternal round" (1 Nephi 10:19; Alma 7:20; 37:12; D&C 3:2; 35:1). We mortals sometimes experience boredom in the routine repetition of our mortal tasks, including even good works; and thus vulnerable, we are urged not to grow weary in well doing (Galatians 6:9; D&C 64:33; 84:80; Alma 37:34). But given God's divine love, there is no boredom on His part amid His repetitive work, for his course, though one eternal round, involves continuous redemption for His children; it is full of goodness and mercy as His long-suffering shows His love in action. In fact we cannot even comprehend the infinite blessings which await the faithful—"eye hath not seen, nor ear heard . . ." (1 Corinthians 2:9).

Jesus' self-described moments of a fulness of joy (3 Nephi 17:20; 28:10) include His moments of ministering and their effects on the righteous—products of His doing the Father's will. These are clear indicators of what matters most to Him and to the Father, for they are one in purpose. Just as when we fear, we are not yet made perfect in love (1 John 4:18; Moroni 8:16), so when we are bored or robotic, we are not yet made perfect in love.

God's purposes are fully centered on us (Moses 1:39; 2 Nephi 26:24). Has He not indicated that he remembers even those who cut themselves off from Him? If they return and repent, "I shall heal them," he said (3 Nephi 18:32), and "Come unto me, all ye that labour and are heavy laden, and I will give you rest" (Matthew 11:28). Peter's advice that we cast our cares upon the Lord was given because of the complete adequacy of the Lord's perfected caring and bearing capacity (1 Peter 5:7). He knows those cares and pains first-hand. In the process of the Atonement, the Lord has known them already (Alma 7:11–12; 2 Nephi 9:21)! His capacity to succor us has already been demonstrated and perfected!

However, *our* bearing capacity clearly is not fully developed. Though we cannot discern all the purposes and meaning in all life's situations, we can with Nephi rely upon this assurance: "I know that [God] loveth his children; nevertheless, I do not know the meaning of all things" (1 Nephi 11:17).

It is so vital, therefore, for us to have faith in the infinite goodness of God, including faith in His timing, faith in His bearing capacity, faith in His mercy, faith in His empathy, and faith in His plans for mankind.

In fulfilling His role in the infinite atonement so crucial to us all, the Savior submissively accepted outrageous indignities. For example, He whose spittle gave a blind man sight was spat upon. New Testament references affirm it, and Book of Mormon prophets anticipated it:

> And the world, because of their iniquity, shall judge him to be a thing of naught; wherefore they scourge him, and he suffereth it; and they smite him, and he suffereth it. Yea, they spit upon him, and he suffereth it, because of his loving kindness and his long-suffering towards the children of men (1 Nephi 19:9).

Jesus was mocked and cruelly scourged, as affirmed in New Testament references but also in other verses: "And thus the flesh becoming subject to the Spirit, or the Son to the Father, being one God, suffereth temptation, and yieldeth not to the temptation, but suffereth himself to be mocked, and scourged, and cast out, and disowned by his people" (Mosiah 15:5).

Various verses give us a scriptural lens with which to view how "in that he himself hath suffered being tempted, he is able to succour them that are tempted" (Hebrews 2:18; see also Mosiah 3:7; Alma 7:11).

In modern revelation we are advised that the remarkable Savior "suffered temptations but gave no heed unto them" (D&C 20:22). In this and other respects, it is said, "There is none like [Him]" for He worked the infinite atonement (Isaiah 46:9).

Scriptures written before Jesus' mortal messiahship carry much accurate anticipation: "He is despised and rejected of men; a man of sorrows, and acquainted with grief: and we hid as it were our faces from him; he was despised, and we esteemed him not" (Isaiah 53:3).

The anticipatory scriptures in the Book of Mormon plainly describe what Jesus would bear in terms of tremendous sorrow and grief:

> And he shall go forth, suffering pains and afflictions and temptations of every kind; and this that the word might be fulfilled which saith he will take upon him the pains and the sicknesses of his people.
>
> And he will take upon him death, that he may loose the bands of death which bind his people; and he will take upon him their infirmities, that his bowels may be filled with mercy, according to the flesh, that he may know according to the flesh how to succor his people according to their infirmities (Alma 7:11–12).

He who bore them all can thus help us empathetically in the midst of our own finite infirmities: "Likewise the Spirit also helpeth our infirmities: for we know not what we should pray for as we ought: but the Spirit itself maketh intercession for us with groanings [sighings] which cannot be uttered" (Romans 8:26).

Jesus' empathy came not alone from the infinite atonement but also as a result of His personal experiences.

For we have not an high priest which cannot be touched with the feeling of our infirmities; but was in all points tempted like as we are, yet without sin (Hebrews 4:15).

In all their afflictions he was afflicted. And the angel of his presence saved them; and in his love, and in his pity, he redeemed them, and bore them, and carried them all the days of old (D&C 133:53).

What the Nephite prophets declared is confirmed by the Lord himself in modern revelation:

For, behold, the Lord your Redeemer suffered death in the flesh; wherefore he suffered the pain of all men, that all men might repent and come unto him (D&C 18:11).

Which suffering caused myself, even God, the greatest of all, to tremble because of pain, and to bleed at every pore, and to suffer both body and spirit—and would that I might not drink the bitter cup, and shrink (D&C 19:18).

When among the Nephites, the resurrected Jesus referred to the experience of drinking that bitter cup:

And behold, I am the light and the life of the world; and I have drunk out of that bitter cup which the Father hath given me, and have glorified the Father in taking upon me the sins of the world, in the which I have suffered the will of the Father in all things from the beginning (3 Nephi 11:11).

If we are to become like Him, we must take His yoke upon us in order to learn of Him who atoned for "the very vilest of sinners" (Mosiah 28:4). "For as the sufferings of Christ abound in us, so our consolation also aboundeth by Christ" (2 Corinthians 1:5).

The joy made possible through the infinite atonement is infinite joy—joy that extends endlessly and to immeasurable heights. Regardless of which dimension of the atonement is pondered, it is wondrously infinite.

Yet unless we are submissive enough to repent and thereafter make His will our guide and director, His suffering for us will not be fully beneficial. Therefore it is crucial for us to develop enough faith to repent, which is surely part of yielding to God's will.

5

"Faith Unto Repentance"

One of the great blessings of real faith in Jesus Christ is that it gives us enough strength and courage to repent. This is called "faith unto repentance" (Alma 34:16–17). The sad truth is that many do not have enough faith to repent, not enough trust in God to change their lifestyles in order to meet emancipating gospel requirements.

The process of repentance involves not only avoiding certain things or desisting from certain practices but also doing positive things. For the latter, we need faith in order to initiate and to sustain better behavior, such as learning to love those we do not like. The life which remains unrefined is evidence of a lack of faith (1 John 5:18; Moroni 8:16).

Understandably, therefore, prophets spend much of their lifetimes both encouraging people to increase faith (Luke 17:5) and decrying certain evils. The very acts of calling our attention to the ultimate choices between captivity and misery on the one hand and liberty and joy on the other illustrate how genuine prophets are about joy. They simply cannot ignore the multitudes walking in the broad way toward the

wide gate (Matthew 7:13). While prophets care too much to
let these souls go unwarned (see 2 Nephi 1:13; Helaman
5:12), they are men of considerable compassion. Witness
Enoch's weeping and pleading for the wicked, Abraham's
pleading for Sodom and Gomorrah, and ancient Joseph's wor-
rying and weeping over his posterity, as made known in the
blessing of Joseph Smith, Senior, to his son Joseph Smith, the
Prophet.

These men resemble Him whose prophets they are. Long
ago, before He was Jesus of Nazareth, the Master pleaded with
the Father to send the gospel to the disobedient in the spirit
prison, the very wicked who would defy Him as Jehovah in
the days of Noah (see Moses 7:39).

His prophets—who spend time proclaiming, affirming,
and building faith, trying to draw us toward real liberty and
real happiness—understand more than others do the Master's
lamentation "O Jerusalem . . ." (Matthew 23:37).

As we look at the misbehavior we see in each of us, we see
both aberrations and preoccupations. Preoccupations can be
a sign that some things have come to mean too much to us.
Though not necessarily bad in itself, a preoccupation can
exercise dominion over us. But whether obsessions, rationalizations, or preoccupations, each is a diversion. Messes of
pottage (Genesis 25:29–34) respond to the "now" in us,
whereas only the submissive heart and mind sees eternity's
considerations.

The Jerusalem of Lehi's time, for example, was seen differently by different eyes. Laman and Lemuel, reluctant to
leave, resented their exodus, saying later, "we have suffered in
the wilderness, which time . . . we might have been happy"

back in the land of Jerusalem (1 Nephi 17:21). Yet not only did the Prophet Lehi see wickedness in the people of Jerusalem but so did Jeremiah. Jeremiah's writings describe the adultery and immorality in the Jerusalem of that time, using imagery about individuals going "by troops in the harlots' houses" (Jeremiah 5:7–8). Laman and Lemuel looked beyond the mark:

> And we know that the people who were in the land of Jerusalem were a righteous people; for they kept the statutes and judgments of the Lord, and all his commandments, according to the law of Moses; wherefore, we know that they are a righteous people; and our father hath judged them, and hath led us away because we would hearken unto his words; yea, and our brother is like unto him. And after this manner of language did my brethren murmur and complain against us (1 Nephi 17:22).

Thus can people come to have errant pride in the status quo; hence the importance of listening to the Lord's prophets without being offended.

Despite all their warnings and pleadings the prophets recognize and honor human agency as given by the God they serve. They are well aware of how dangerous the sensual human appetites are, but also are conscious that these celebrated appetites of the "here and now" will not survive after the resurrection, for "the world passeth away, and the lust thereof" (1 John 2:17). The worldly appetites are, in a sense, like secularism's manna, a day-to-day thing, seldom preserved overnight. Instead, prophets urge the long view of the individual's eternal self-interest.

To have the faith to deny oneself certain of life's questionable pleasures is to affirm oneself, an attitude involving a healthy self-respect that is proper for the submissive. One's intrinsic, eternal worth is not to be traded for the things of the moment. Jesus made it clear that we are to deny ourselves the things of the flesh as part of taking up the cross daily (3 Nephi 12:30; Luke 9:23). Actually, to cease sinning is to begin living. True repentance involves turning fully away from those things which are wrong and turning fully to God (Ezekiel 18:30), an act impossible without faith. Though such obedience is voluntary, it is obedience still.

Such obedience is not blind, however, but instead flows comprehendingly from faith:

> Repentance, the second principle of the gospel, follows naturally in the life of one who has faith in Jesus Christ. One who learns about the gospel, who receives a testimony and develops faith in it, soon recognizes that his manner of living does not meet the conditions upon which the promised blessings are predicated. Such a realization creates in him a godly sorrow and a desire to reform his life and be forgiven for his former sins and transgressions. Repentance is the means by which such a person qualifies himself for the cleansing power of forgiveness, which heals his soul.[1]

For a person to take up his cross means "to deny himself all ungodliness, and every worldly lust, and keep my commandments" (JST, Matthew 16:26). Such daily discipline would be impossible without faith unto both avoidance and repentance.

Thoughtful observers note how powerful an influence environmental conditions can be—good and bad. Likewise, no wise individual would want to diminish the shaping significance of an individual's genetic inheritance. Even so, adverse environmental experiences need not be automatically perpetuated. It is possible to break the chain of events by saying, "Let it stop with me!" Or, with regard to wiser patterns of behavior and living, one can assert, "Let them *start* with me!" We see such heroism about us all the time. While we must always begin from where we are, we need not stay where we are.

Familial patterns of abuse and unrighteous parental dominion obviously affect us profoundly. But these need not enslave future generations. Deprivation does not mean automatic and perpetual ruination. Emancipation is possible. God can heal us, if we will submit to him. This is not to diminish the degree of difficulty encountered in bringing about desired change, but in that very difficulty lies the need for faith and patience. In any event, we are not compelled by forces outside ourselves to give up or to give in. If there is to be a surrender, let it be to Him who loves us and can help us—not a shoulder-shrugging salute to circumstance.

Those who live in homes where cutting criticism of the Church is "in the air" will find it much harder to be grounded in the gospel. But victims can emancipate themselves from that error, as from all others, by a trust in our loving Father and obedience to His wishes.

As noted, true repentance means both turning away from

bad patterns *and* turning to God. If the full process does not occur, individuals will find themselves experiencing the enervating "sorrowing of the damned" (Mormon 2:13). Or they will slip back into well-worn past patterns.

In the absence of faith unto repentance and therefore of submissiveness, there is resistance to the Spirit, to wise counsel, and to the instructive feedback which flows from life itself. Resistance to the Spirit can, for instance, reflect fascination with the praise of the world or with those things which provide joy for a season. Unsubmissive selfishness, by way of example, encourages us to travel light by jettisoning commitments, gaining the illusion of being unencumbered while actually being plunged ever more rapidly towards that sobering solitariness which is selfishness at the end of its journey.

The resentment towards the messenger of repentance quite naturally reflects a lack of faith. Perhaps, too, the counsel is disregarded because the messenger is imperfect. Whatever the case, without faith the hearers will deflect—sometimes deftly and clearly—the invitations to turn back to God. Those who err do not usually want to disturb the flow of life's pleasures or to question their seeming self-sufficiency. This latter attitude was noted in words revealed to the Apostle John that described the distorted self-sufficiency of some who declared, "I am rich, and increased with goods, and have need of nothing" (Revelation 3:17).

In the process of our enduring chastening, which is so often a distasteful part of repentance, the chastening can come to us from circumstances (Helaman 12:3) or from counsel. The righteous as well as the wicked are liable to be chastened, as in the case of the brother of Jared, who apparently had not prayed as regularly as he should: "And it came to pass at the end of four years that the Lord came again unto the brother of Jared, and stood in a cloud and talked with him. And for the space of three hours did the Lord talk with the brother of Jared, and chastened him because he remembered not to call upon the name of the Lord" (Ether 2:14).

Sometimes our chastening comes to us compressed in a difficult "little season" (D&C 103:4). Whatever the case, if we cannot endure chastening we do not yet qualify as true disciples: "My people must be tried in all things, that they may be prepared to receive the glory that I have for them, even the glory of Zion; and he that will not bear chastisement is not worthy of my kingdom" (D&C 136:31).

Being such a premier virtue, submissiveness is not to be mastered in a moment, once and for all. Hence the need for patience on the part of those of us who, while falling short of keeping all the Lord's commandments, truly "seeketh so to do" (D&C 46:9).

Underneath our rationalizations, usually, is a deep destitution enclosed in profound pride. Pride, at its core, involves a measure of self-worship, however mild. After all, we are to "have no other God" before the real God, including self-pleasing and self-worship. If we are really keeping the first commandment, we will worship him sufficiently to want to be more and more like Him.

George MacDonald laid bare the half-heartedness of some of us: "'I cannot be perfect; it is hopeless; and He does not expect it.'—It would be more honest if he said, 'I do not want to be perfect: I am content to be saved.' Such as he do not care for being perfect as their Father in heaven is perfect, but for being what they called saved."[2]

Selfishness is so insistently preemptive:

> In those days there was no king in Israel: every man did that which was right in his own eyes (Judges 21:25).

> They seek not the Lord to establish his righteousness, but every man walketh in his own way, and after the image of his own god (D&C 1:16).

Too many, if only silently, say with Pharaoh, "Who is the Lord, that I should obey his voice?" (Exodus 5:2).

In their resentment, those who worry that someone will "rule over" them rationalize their resistance to repentance. They resist because they are already well along in self-pleasing. Ironically, even as they fret about being ruled over, they are actually being ruled over by an aristocracy of appetites or by the stern sovereignty of selfishness. "There is one kind of religion in which the more devoted a man is, the fewer proselytes he makes: the worship of himself."[3]

Others say they would consider having faith in God if only he would meet their demands. "Why will he not show himself unto us?" (Helaman 16:18).

Isaiah Berlin has called "the central question of politics—the question of obedience and coercion. 'Why should I obey anyone else?'"[4] Increasingly in the modern world there are those who see no reason to obey anyone or anything—including God, unless God submits Himself to their demands.

In biblical terms, "to obey" is equated with "to hear." It is assumed that when we really hear the word of God we will obey it (Deuteronomy 5:27). This was Nephi's form of obedience: "I will go and do . . ." (1 Nephi 3:7).

Hearing, really hearing, will bring obeying. Those who are thus submissive are not content to "live by bread alone" but instead live "by every word that proceedeth out of the mouth of the Lord" (Deuteronomy 8:3; Matthew 4:4).

This attunement to the word of the Lord reflects progressive and deepening discipleship. "And by hearkening to observe all the words which I, the Lord their God, shall speak unto them, they shall never cease to prevail until the kingdoms of the world are subdued under my feet, and the earth is given unto the saints, to possess it forever and ever" (D&C 103:7).

When the Lord describes His divine style of leadership (as in Doctrine and Covenants section 121), it is clear that our submissiveness is to be given voluntarily. It is brought about by God's loving, long-suffering persuasion. His method of ruling over us is "with a rod of iron" (Revelation 2:27), but the rod of iron is "the word of God" (1 Nephi 15:23–24).

God desires to lead us by truths, principles, and laws. Furthermore, He desires us to have our own personal verification of the rightness of His ways, even though they are not man's ways (Isaiah 55:8–9). But first we must hear His word. We cannot evaluate His higher ways using the criteria of man's lower ways. God will give us the verification of His ways, and we can know that His ways are good (Alma 32).

On the other hand, there can be comfortable but unjustified pride in routine and in customary ways which everyone assumes to be all right. "Notwithstanding they believed in a Great Spirit, they supposed that whatsoever they did was right" (Alma 18:5). This pattern tends to emerge when the scriptural memory has been severed.

We see another variation, the "eat, drink, and be merry" philosophy (2 Nephi 28:7; see also Proverbs 16:25). Consequences come both quickly and slowly in the lives of individuals and of whole societies. Sometimes scarcely one generation passes before some consequences appear. Other consequences slumber like a silent virus, ready to take a later toll.

Our defiance of God is an expression of our ignorance, not of our individuality. Peter warned lapsing Church members about the need to avoid shaping their lives according to their former lusts (1 Peter 1:14). Instead, disciples should be shaping their lives to become even as the Father and the Son are.

It should not surprise us, therefore, that it takes faith to repent; faith not only that God lives but also that He really knows what is best for us and, in fact, that He really desires us to become like Him in order to share in His joy and happiness. A passive belief in a distant, undemanding God neither stirs the soul nor changes wrong behavioral patterns. Belief in a vague "life force" somewhere in space does not open the windows of the mind to the "truth . . . of things as they really are, and of things as they really will be" (Jacob 4:13).

Faith and repentance are clearly and continuously interactive, the one virtue enhancing the other: "You must repent . . . even until ye shall have faith in Christ, . . . and . . . the cloud of darkness shall be removed from overshadowing you" (Helaman 5:41).

We read, for instance, of a very distinguished group of

individuals who had been "ordained . . . on account of their faith *and repentance*" (Alma 13:10, emphasis added). Good, but still imperfect, they were full of faith, but also of repentance. The process is the same for all of us, and it carries such rich promises:

> Yea, he that repenteth and exerciseth faith, and bringeth forth good works, and prayeth continually without ceasing—unto such it is given to know the mysteries of God; yea, unto such it shall be given to reveal things which never have been revealed; yea, and it shall be given unto such to bring thousands of souls to repentance, even as it has been given unto us to bring these our brethren to repentance (Alma 26:22).

A turning unto God brings forth appropriate works "meet for repentance" (Acts 26:20), which the submissive gladly place on the altar. Hence through his prophets Jesus urges people to bring forth "fruits meet for repentance" (Matthew 3:8).

Some come suddenly to a realization of their awful sins, as did Judas: "Then Judas, which had betrayed him, when he saw that he was condemned, repented himself, and brought again the thirty pieces of silver to the chief priests and elders" (Matthew 27:3).

Others are troubled by the status quo—sufficiently troubled unto sincere inquiry:

> And the king said unto them: Arise, for I will grant unto you your lives, and I will not suffer that ye shall be my servants; but I will insist that ye shall administer unto

me; for I have been somewhat troubled in mind because
of the generosity and the greatness of the words of thy
brother Ammon; and I desire to know the cause why he
has not come up out of Middoni with thee (Alma 22:3).

Being troubled can produce resolution and repentance:
"And now, my son, I desire that ye should let these things
trouble you no more, and only let your sins trouble you, with
that trouble which shall bring you down unto repentance"
(Alma 42:29).

Events too can humble us, producing feelings which may
be productive of repentance: "In the day of their peace they
esteemed lightly my counsel; but, in the day of their trouble,
of necessity they feel after me" (D&C 101:8).

Significantly, God's long-suffering is the very means of
His providing us with time or "space" within which to repent.
It was so even in the beginning:

> For behold, if Adam had put forth his hand imme-
> diately, and partaken of the tree of life, he would have
> lived forever, according to the word of God, having no
> space for repentance; yea, and also the word of God
> would have been void, and the great plan of salvation
> would have been frustrated (Alma 42:5).

It has been so since then:

> And the days of the children of men were pro-
> longed, according to the will of God, that they might
> repent while in the flesh; wherefore, their state became a
> state of probation, and their time was lengthened,

according to the commandments which the Lord God gave unto the children of men (2 Nephi 2:21).

There was a space granted unto man in which he might repent; therefore this life became a probationary state; a time to prepare to meet God; a time to prepare for that endless state which has been spoken of by us, which is after the resurrection of the dead (Alma 12:24).

Unfortunately this precious additional time and opportunity often go unutilized: "I gave her space to repent of her fornication; and she repented not" (Revelation 2:21).

Real intent and real sincerity are required for real repentance (Mosiah 26:29). One indication of genuine repentance is whether we confess our sins and then forsake them (D&C 58:43). If godly sorrow occurs within us, it is a sign of real concern that we may have offended God. On the other hand, worldly sorrow that we feel simply because we have been caught or inconvenienced is not sufficient for repentance. Not turning all the way to God can create a terrible trap:

> But behold this my joy was vain, for their sorrowing was not unto repentance, because of the goodness of God; but it was rather the sorrowing of the damned, because the Lord would not always suffer them to take happiness in sin.
>
> And they did not come unto Jesus with broken hearts and contrite spirits, but they did curse God, and wish to die. Nevertheless they would struggle with the sword for their lives (Mormon 2:13–14).

Sooner or later we must all either repent or suffer (D&C 19:4). God wants to spare us that form of suffering.

When we are struggling to learn to love, we can have faith in God's developmental plans for others as well as for ourselves. Then we do not feel threatened by those who are our superiors or who are becoming such. The more unselfish we are, the more able we are to find joy in their successes, all the while rejoicing without comparing. In any case, our only valid spiritual competition is with our old selves, not with each other. True love and friendship enable us to keep that perspective. The things about other people that truly matter are their qualities such as love, mercy, justice, and patience, and their service to others. The things that matter much less—style, appearance, and mannerisms—become comparatively unimportant. Finally, our capacity to be meek and lowly enough to love without requiring reciprocity is enhanced by our coming to know how much we are loved by Jesus, even when we do not return His love as we might.

Of this mortal developmental process, which requires so much ongoing repentance, the rhetorical question might be asked, "Is there not another way?" But we are clearly told that the Lord's name and God's plan are the only way. The answer, therefore, is a stark "No!" "And now, behold, my beloved brethren, this is the way; and there is none other way nor name given under heaven whereby man can be saved in the kingdom of God" (2 Nephi 31:21).

With regard to human suffering, for instance, there is no way in which the misery caused by misused agency could be removed without removing agency. Nor can the necessary developing experiences and examinations be removed from this mortal school. Of course we should seek to alleviate all the forms of human suffering we can.

But while not all forms of suffering are removable, we can eliminate that suffering caused by our sins if we are submissive enough to do so.

How could we have a greater promise than this?

> O ye fair ones, how could ye have departed from the ways of the Lord! O ye fair ones, how could ye have rejected that Jesus, who stood with open arms to receive you (Mormon 6:17)!

How could we have a Lord more ready to forgive?

> Come now, and let us reason together, saith the Lord: though your sins be as scarlet, they shall be as white as snow; though they be red like crimson, they shall be as wool (Isaiah 1:18).

> All his transgressions that he hath committed, they shall not be mentioned unto him: in his righteousness that he hath done he shall live (Ezekiel 18:22).

> Behold, he who has repented of his sins, the same is forgiven, and I, the Lord, remember them no more (D&C 58:42).

First, however, we must heed His word sufficiently to develop faith to repent. For the intellectually meek, Joseph Smith promised:

> Every word that proceedeth from the mouth of Jehovah has such an influence over the human mind the

logical mind that it is convincing without other testimony. Faith cometh by hearing.[5]

So much of the hesitancy to repent occurs because it takes
"faith unto repentance," which faith cannot be developed
when we reject the doctrines, ordinances, and covenants of the
gospel. Some actually are offended by the gospel's theological
simplicity. Some think to blur their accountability for truth
by disregarding it or by saying they do not believe it. Some
reason that if it should turn out that there is a God, He will
be harmlessly indulgent:

> And there shall also be many which shall say: Eat,
> drink, and be merry; nevertheless, fear God—he will
> justify in committing a little sin; yea, lie a little, take the
> advantage of one because of his words, dig a pit for thy
> neighbor; there is no harm in this; and do all these
> things, for tomorrow we die; and if it so be that we are
> guilty, God will beat us with a few stripes, and at last we
> shall be saved in the kingdom of God (2 Nephi 28:8).

Withdrawal and denial are painful, hence we put off full
repentance: "When a man begins to abstain, then first he rec-
ognizes the strength of his passion."[6]

Even when faith is present, unless we are settled and submissive faith can be quickly shattered by confronting circumstances. It can also be slowly eroded by time, if neglected. The
passage of time works against faith, if only as a function of the
dominance of the cares of the world, unless faith is being con-
stantly nourished. Whether one is looking forward to the
coming of the Messiah, as many did for many centuries, or

looking backward over many centuries to His mortal Messiahship, it matters little, for the challenge is the same. Faith is essential in both situations. Those who think it would have been easier in the meridian of time should remember the excusing attitude of "Is not this the carpenter's son?" (Matthew 13:55) and the disdain of some of Jesus' relatives and kinsmen who did not "believe in Him" and may even have dissembled to get Him "out of town" (John 7:1–5).

Trying to live without God in the world delivers us over to the grinding dominance of the world. Sufficient faith unto repentance does not arise amid such choking cares. Korihor's cynical but articulate conclusion was "Yea, . . . their traditions and their dreams and their whims and their visions and their pretended mysteries" exist because they do not wish to "offend some unknown being, who they say is God—a being who never has been seen or known, who never was nor ever will be" (Alma 30:28). Whereas Pharaoh said he knew not God (Exodus 5:2), Korihor went much further. In both cases, willful ignorance took its toll.

Counsel, including advice to repent, is not naturally easy to bear. The more accurate, the more painful. We have been instructed before criticizing someone else for having a mote in his eye to see if we have a beam in our own (Matthew 7:3). We have also been advised to show forth increased love to the object of reproof (D&C 121:43).

We need also to be careful about being too quick to complain about institutional and individual imperfections in the Church. For instance, before we complain about someone else's insensitivity or errant authoritarianism, we need to examine meekly our own leadership style. It would be well to accept too that in a church which oversees some of the processes of repentance, inevitably this perfect and emancipating doctrine is sometimes imperfectly administered.

Life in the Church means experiencing leaders who are not always wise, mature, and deft. In fact, some of us are as bumpy and uneven as a sackful of old doorknobs. Some of the polishing we experience is a result of grinding against each other. How vital submissiveness is in such circumstances, especially if the lubrication of love is not amply present.

In a church established, among other reasons, for the perfecting of the Saints—an ongoing process—it is naive to expect, and certainly unfair to demand, perfection in our peers. A brief self-inventory is wise before we "cast the first stone." Possessing a few rocks in our own heads, it is especially dangerous to have rocks too ready in our hands.

Our capacity as Church members to love and to forgive will be freshly and severely tested as battered and bruised souls come into the Church in ever-larger numbers. Some come in from the cold shivering. Others are breathless, having caught what was for them the last train out of Babylon. Their own continued process of repentance will be much aided if they see, all about them, more regular emphasis in the lives of the rest of us on faith unto repentance.

The personal risks of being in the world are real and constant. Nevertheless, "for this cause" came we "unto this hour" (John 12:27), the hour of our own mortal experience. Will we too live righteously and submissively, as did He?

The adversary seeks to lead us carefully down to hell, whereas it is the steep road of repentance which we are pledged to travel. Lucifer is an expert at giving the guided tour, studiously avoiding jarring us into spiritual sensibility during the gradual descent. He can blur the passing landscape so adroitly that we scarcely notice leaving the mountains, and then the uplands, as we are headed toward the slums and, finally, arrive at dockside on the gulf of misery.

Sometimes being worn down is our own fault for not providing space and time for ourselves for spiritual renewal, an area that to the adversary is "off limits." We need the equivalent of designated nonsmoking areas to secure us from secondhand sensuality, inappropriate humor, twisted film, and bad music.

As to our circumstances, the Lord has promised He will either make a way to escape or a way to bear adversity (1 Corinthians 10:13). As to temptation, most of the time there is an obvious way to escape, but prevention—not being enticed in the first place—is more sure and is part of having sufficient faith.

There is no other way for us to overcome the world (John 16:33; D&C 76:53) unless we live in the world. While in it, we have been repeatedly warned about the diverting and addicting nature of riches, power, and praise. The warning phrase "the eye of a needle," with regard to the risk of riches, along with the "almost all" phrase concerning the abuse of authority and power, are stern warnings indeed (Matthew 19:24; D&C 121:39).

Some of the misuses of power, against which we are warned, occur when we seek "to gratify" our sins. Why? Because open admission of our sins would fray still further the legitimacy to which we may tenaciously cling.

We are not to gratify our pride. Why? Because it is the

antithesis of submission to God's will. Because the gospel asks us insistently to be meek and lowly, as Jesus was. Pride needs to be starved, not fed. Moreover, whose needs should we be trying to meet? "The Son of man," even, "came not to be ministered unto, but to minister" (Matthew 20:28). The Father Himself is giving His full time and all His perfected talents to "bring to pass the immortality and eternal life of man" (Moses 1:39). What are *we* doing? We should take care that we are not merely "straightening deck chairs on the Titanic."

We are warned, too, that we must not gratify our vain ambitions (D&C 121:37). Why? Whose purposes are we truly seeking, ours or His? Compared to God's, what would our full, extrapolated agenda, open and hidden, look like if fully exposed?

We are told we should not exercise compulsion or dominion in any unrighteous degree over the souls of men (D&C 121:37–39). Why? If He who is all-wise and all-loving shuns compulsion, dare we use it? Whose style should we be emulating, anyway?

By developing faith enough to know "who" we are and "why" we are here, we can better resist the tempting taunt, "Why not?" and the devilishly democratic, "Everybody does it!" If we know the realities of "things as they really are," we will view daily life differently. Deciding and acting out of eternal considerations, we can keep this mortal micro-dot in perspective. Jesus' disciples are *not* like everybody else.

Shallow commitment brings no faith unto repentance and no introduction to "the deep things of God" (1 Corinthians 2:10). For instance, if we assault our ears with sounds which are not truly music, by that practice we are losing our capacity to distinguish beautiful music from other sounds, lumping all sounds into that "compound in one." High-quality music is so desperately needed to counteract secular sounds. Brigham Young once said, "There is no music in hell," doubtless a correct statement as to real music. But some sounds masquerading as music today belong naturally to that grim place; and they would further qualify that awful place for its designation.

So many in the world regard the assertion of self as the essential verification of self, that is, the hot pursuit of appetites proves that one really exists. But by so proving that "I am," we move ever further away from the real "I AM"—Jehovah. He submitted Himself from the beginning, saying, "Here am I, send me" (Abraham 3:27), and saying later, "Not what I will, but what thou wilt" (Mark 14:36). To the extent that we live under the arrogant aristocracy of appetites, there can be no exercising of faith unto repentance. Appetites demand their own calisthenics.

It was He, the keenest of all intellects ever to grace this planet, who humbly said, "My doctrine is not mine but his that sent me" (John 7:16) and, "There is none good but one, that is, God" (Matthew 19:17). It was meek Jesus who honored Adam when He came so gracefully to that very special "family home evening" (D&C 107:53–57). There is such supernal grace in His submissiveness!

Even after all the careful, wise, premortal tutorials, the only way to tame the raw self with finality was to place it in a mortal environment. Therein we are free to choose. Therein we can experience the sour and the sweet. Therein we learn about consequences. This process is the only way to bring about final and fundamental changes, even in those who are spiritually submissive.

If one has any doubt about how enormous ego is, he need only look at history. How often history turns upon collisions and intrusions of ego: Lucifer's bid for power in the premortal existence; Cain's bid for ascendancy over Abel; Lucifer's pleading for Moses to worship him; Jacob and Esau's earlier jousting over place; David's apparent feeling, despite loyal Uriah, that the burdens of leadership were such that he deserved Bathsheba; Laman and Lemuel's refusing to be "ruled over" by Nephi; the anxious mother of James and John seeking next-world ascendancy for them; and the rejection of Abinadi, the prophet, by a society who felt he had no business telling them what to do, just as in ancient Israel when some rebelled against Moses.

In all these and in episodes like them in our daily lives we see ego at work, refusing to give place for faith unto repentance.

Submissiveness to the Lord and to His purposes may be the last thing most of us achieve, if we achieve it at all. When whatever dominion is to come does come in the next world, it will come to those of demonstrated faith—flowing *without compulsory means* forever and ever (D&C 121:46).

Little wonder that the prophets are so repetitious in their warnings, some almost shrill at times. After all, if one were permitted only a few final lines—words to be transmitted to family, friends, and posterity—they might very reasonably take the form of headlines or a shouted summation to those not stirred by the still, small voice. In this spirit the Prophet Joseph Smith said:

Oh, that I could snatch them from the vortex of misery, into which I behold them plunging themselves, by their sins; that I might be enabled by the warning voice, to be an instrument of bringing them to unfeigned repentance, that they might have faith to stand in the evil day![7]

Meanwhile, the drama on the human stage goes on in near-perpetual reenactment. Even after victory, personal or national, unless we are submissive we are so likely to resume the follies of the past. Unless we are meek and lowly enough to repent, we will fail to understand that "none is acceptable before God, save the meek and lowly in heart" (Moroni 7:44). If we are submissive, He can do so much more with us and through us.

George MacDonald wrote:

For He regards men not as they are merely, but as they shall be; . . . as they are now growing, or capable of growing, toward that image after which He made them that they might grow to it. Therefore a thousand stages, each in itself all but valueless, are of inestimable worth as the necessary and connected gradations of an infinite progress. A condition which of declension would indicate a devil, may of growth indicate a saint.[8]

In the closing years of the twentieth century man's follies so closely resemble the follies of centuries past, but on a grander scale. Nations engage in arms races with the foolish rationalization that the outcome of *this* race will really be different. Individuals, full of selfishness and self-pity, engage in adultery, child abuse, and other forms of sexual immorality. Many mortals are still kept in bondage of one form or another, racial, political, and financial; in fact, massive debt mortgages posterity's tomorrows, adding to the growing sense of hopelessness.

Nations continue their costly and obsessive work on the Maginot Line of materialism, looking to it for satisfaction and safety even as they are being outflanked by racing columns of consequences. The various streamlets converge into complexity and futility, leading to that time, foretold by Jesus, when there will be "distress of nations, with perplexity" (Luke 21:25). The tragedy goes on—for the umpteenth time on the stage of human history!

We have been warned that there is a law irrevocably decreed upon which all blessings are predicated (D&C 130:20–21). In the ecology of heaven, there is a counterpart: we receive the decreed misery which flows from the violation of those same laws, unless we have sufficient faith to repent. Deathbed repentance is better than none at all, but it is not what the Lord desires, because "it is the will of God that man should repent & serve him in health & in the strength & power of his mind in order to secure his blessings & not wait untill he is called to die."[9]

Early repentance thus permits earlier and more extensive service.

God has rich blessings which He is anxious to bestow upon us. "All hearts must repent—be pure and God will . . . bless them in a manner that could not be bless'd in any other way."[10]

Redemptiveness should ever be our aim and persuasive long-suffering our style. Joseph Smith said:

> Nothing is so much calculated to lead people to forsake sin as to take them by the hand and watch over them with tenderness. When persons manifest the least kindness and love to me, O what pow'r it has over my mind, while the opposite course has a tendency to harrow up all the harsh feelings and depress the human mind. . . . The nearer we get to our heavenly Father the more are we disposed to look with compassion on perishing souls to take them upon our shoulders and cast their sins behind our back.[11]

The meekly repentant can avoid the trap cited by the Prophet Joseph: "We are full of selfishness—the devil flatters us that we are very righteous, while we are feeding on the faults of others."[12]

He who would bless us, though omnipotent, must nevertheless wait upon us; it is we who must move first. "His heart is glad when thou doest arise and say, 'I will go to my Father.' . . . Bethink thee of something that thou oughtest to do, and go to do it, if it be but the sweeping of a room, or the preparing of a meal, or a visit to a friend. Heed not thy feeling: Do thy work."[13]

God delights in the first signs of righteous change: "What father is not pleased with the first tottering attempt of his little one to walk? What father would be satisfied with anything but the manly step of the full-grown son?"[14]

If we will submit, we will mirror the Master more

faithfully. "The self is given to us that we may sacrifice it: it is ours, that we, like Christ, may have somewhat to offer."[15]

It takes time to prepare for eternity, and sin wastes vital time.

As the Prophet Joseph testified, we cannot arrive spiritually "in a moment":

> God has created man with a mind capable of instruction, and a faculty which may be enlarged in proportion to the heed and diligence given to the light communicated from heaven to the intellect; and that the nearer man approaches perfection, the clearer are his views, and the greater his enjoyments, till he has overcome the evils of his life and lost every desire for sin; and like the ancients, arrives at that point of faith where he is wrapped in the power and glory of his Maker and is caught up to dwell with Him. But we consider that this is a station to which no man ever arrived in a moment: he must have been instructed in the government and laws of that kingdom by proper degrees, until his mind is capable in some measure of comprehending the propriety, justice, equality, and consistency of the same.[16]

While sins are individual, their accumulations have macro consequences. Take for example lying—breaching the ninth and other commandments (Exodus 20:16; Leviticus 19:11). As Walt Harrington pointed out, when deceit becomes common so does distrust, especially in the "big anonymous monster we call modern life," wherein "anonymity breeds contempt." "Because we live and work in what seems ever unraveling and befuddling complexity today, disbelief has seeped into every corner of daily life."[17] This latter observation recalls Jesus' prophecy about latter-day "distress of nations, with perplexity" (Luke 21:25). It recalls, too, Nephi's prophecy about the last days, when "many" would "lie a little" and "take the advantage of one because of his words" (2 Nephi 28:8).

Relative ethics provide no cure, since these may merely urge, in Paul Ekman's words, "Don't lie to anyone you want to have a continuing relationship with," so if you don't care about a lasting relationship, "truth is no big deal."[18] Similar rationalizations have been advanced about sexual immorality and "meaningful" relationships.

Biblical injunctions against lying are numerous and clear. The Restoration scriptures are directive and unequivocal: "Thou shalt not lie; he that lieth and will not repent shall be cast out" (D&C 42:21).

Additionally and importantly, the Restoration brings not only affirmation of divine standards but also needed refreshment in order to hold to these high standards. Establishing our true brotherhood and sisterhood is a much-needed antidote to anonymity. We have a continuing relationship with everybody, with accountability here and in the hereafter. The importance of knowing "who" all of us are amid Father's plan cannot be overstated, because it affects so many things so profoundly.

Yet another illustration of the gospel's relevance is the care of the poor. Modern revelation advises as to the earth's resources: "there is enough and to spare" (D&C 104:17). Governments and economic systems falter before those assurances. Especially sobering is this divine declaration: "But it is not given that one man should possess that which is above another, wherefore the world lieth in sin" (D&C 49:20).

Jesus has clearly answered the question "Who is my neighbor?" (Luke 10:29). Restoration scriptures call upon us to be "willing to bear one another's burdens, that they may be light" (Mosiah 18:8). Furthermore, "every man" is to "esteem his brother as himself" (D&C 38:24).

Such is the gospel's tremendous response—whether to anomie or anonymity!

A "cosmic force" God would not give customized commandments, as to the very rich and righteous man who lacked one thing—the capacity to sell all he had in order to give to the poor (Luke 18:18–24; Matthew 19:16–24; Mark 10:17–25). King Benjamin reminded those of us who are insensitive to the poor, "Are we not all beggars?" (Mosiah 4:19.)

Hard questions were put to the mortal Messiah not only about one's neighbors but also about "what is truth?" (John 18:38.) Jesus' answers, including His Restoration answers, are worthy of pondering: "And truth is knowledge of things as they are, and as they were, and as they are to come" (D&C 93:24; see also 1 Corinthians 2:10; Jacob 4:13).

Most assuredly, these answers respond unequivocally to cynicism and uncertainty. If we know "who" we are, esteeming ourselves as children of God, then we know the true identity of others, esteeming them. If ignorant, we are more likely to use them, abuse them, lie to them, or be blinded to their poverty.

The many forms of adultery, lying, stealing, bearing false witness, coveting, and so on, are stern reminders of what happens when mortals depart from the commandments of God or attempt to rationalize and relativize them. The greatest danger is when we seek to dilute divine doctrines to make them so comfortable that no real repentance is required of us.

When societies' trendy fashions are indulged, such as disposable spouses, frequently the loss of community follows. On the other hand, submission to God's will brings discipleship in the community of God. Men will try in vain to establish their own standards of righteousness "in the likeness of the world," but these efforts "shall perish" (D&C 1:16). This occurs, wrote Paul, because people are "ignorant of God's righteousness," because "they have not submitted themselves unto the righteousness of God" (Romans 10:3).

So we come back to submissiveness once again!

Mortal attempts at substitution would be comic if they were not so tragic. Such efforts are often sincere and even laudable; they even have their own dogmatism amid their relativism. But man's efforts somehow never solve the problem. The Lord's plan when followed does—as with Enoch's city and with the Nephites in the early Christian centuries. Small wonder that, in responding to poverty, the Lord's injunction about maximum effectiveness is that "it must be done in mine own way" (D&C 104:16).

Secular solutions tend to be rehabilitative rather than preventive. Treating one challenge flowing out of the violation of God's spiritual ecology may mean that one problem is "cured," but another will take its place, until . . .

God's ways are truly higher than man's ways (Isaiah 55:9), and we can reap the benefits of that superiority if we will submit. If not, much unnecessary human misery will continue.

The "commandments of men" (D&C 46:7; Colossians 2:22) may seem compelling, but in reality they are lower ways for a lower world.

The need for wise mortal laws was eloquently described by Bolt's Sir Thomas More in *A Man for All Seasons*. When Roper says, "I'd cut down every law in England to do that!" More replies: "And when the last law was down, and the Devil turned round on you—where would you hide, Roper, the laws all being flat? This country's planted thick with laws from coast to coast—man's laws, not God's—and if you cut them down—and you're just the man to do it—d'you really think you could stand upright in the winds that would blow then?"[19]

Where do mortals seek shelter when the laws of God are trampled down?

There is a large difference between choosing to lie, and saying there is no real truth to be served anyway. There is a stark difference between hypocrisy, with its tacit admission of standards, and, on the other hand, saying there are really no standards to be violated.

Those who discount gospel morality by smugly describing it as old-fashioned, understate: it is actually old-old-old-old-old-fashioned morality—going back to the beginning of time and beyond. In contrast, morality born of majoritarianism is risky, especially in times like those of Noah and Sodom. Our eyes and thoughts are, instead, supposed to be upon a far "better country" (Hebrews 11:16).

Patient, persistent discipleship depends upon our continued willingness to submit to Him who would guide us to that country.

6

"Willing to Submit"

As we look at the role of excessive ego on the human scene in the sweep of history, we see how powerful a force ego is. True, there are great moments of human achievement in which persons or nations set aside ego or political pride in order to do what is needed, but these moments are rare and are usually short lived.

Such was the case when the congruent foreign policies of the United States and the Soviet Union—otherwise often adversarial—permitted the formation of modern Israel; in a few months, that brief accord had dissolved. The birth of the United States was possible because of facilitating friendships which fashioned agreements to produce a remarkable constitution and pooled persuasion in its ratification and implementation. The accord did not last long. Alexander Hamilton and James Madison, for instance, who with John Jay produced the persuasive Federalist Papers, had a philosophical and political falling-out not long after the nation had been born.

However great human accomplishments are, they represent but a tithe of what the Lord could help us to achieve on this planet if only we would be meek and lowly, submitting to Him.

In the balancing of things, the different talents of men and women often provide some safety; as often happens in mortal affairs, the sail is played off against the anchor. At the same time, how much more could be done with regard to poverty and disease, for example, if significant international accords could be humbly reached—egos aside! Or if the death-dealing and enslaving patterns of drug addiction were not fed by those whose selfish and corrupt desires for gain prevent real cures!

Submission to God, among many things, requires us to strip ourselves of our pride in order to be obedient to Him. In that process we make ourselves so much more useful in the achievement of God's purposes among His children.

We are much on our guard, however. Often we are frozen into those patterns of behavior and thinking which imprison us, albeit in a well-lit cell. Jesus speaks about setting free the captives, but some captives are so contented that they refuse to leave their cells.

Without faith in God, in His plan of salvation, and in Jesus' infinite atonement, we cannot really submit to and trust in God's perspectives. Nor can we adequately trust in His timing, which we do not fully understand. Nor can we trust in His loving purposes, which are too profound for us to understand fully. Truly we are "confused at the grace which so fully he proffers [us]."[1] Nevertheless we can humbly and gratefully accept it. If sufficiently submissive, too, we can resolve to repent and to become more determined disciples.

Certain supernal spiritual blessings seem to come only

after demonstrated obedience. After Nephi declared, "I will go and do . . ." (1 Nephi 3:7), and then demonstrated his discipleship, he received visions and blessings on the top of exceedingly high mountains (1 Nephi 11:1; 2 Nephi 4:25).

Peter, James, and John would not have been on the Mount of Transfiguration if they had not been obedient and submissive disciples well before that transcendent occasion.

Joseph Smith would have never experienced the marvelous theophany at Palmyra if he had not obeyed James's counsel (James 1:5); he truly desired to know which church to join.

Abraham desired the blessings which had come to his righteous forefathers (Abraham 1:2). He was willing to pay the price, journeying to a place of inheritance, "not knowing whither he went" (Hebrews 11:8).

How powerful a role our true desires play in our lives! Desire both initiates our actions and sustains us—for good or evil. If we desire wealth or power, these will tend to be the moving causes of our actions. If instead we desire spiritual things and are obedient, the promised blessings will come to us. Just as it is not possible to save an individual against his will, so blessings do not come against our wills.

True discipleship is for volunteers only. Only volunteers will trust the Guide sufficiently to follow Him in the dangerous ascent which only He can lead.

Clearly, those who discount spiritual things and do not really desire and seek those things will not receive them. Many such are totally skeptical, their tone perhaps being represented in this declaration: "We find insufficient evidence for belief in the existence of a supernatural; it is either meaningless or irrelevant to the question of the survival and fulfillment of the human race. As non-theists, we begin with humans not God, nature not deity. . . . No deity will save us; we must save ourselves."[2]

Since some prefer any but the real explanation for life's purposes, they will manage to find something on which to focus their desires. For instance, the religion of selfishness is openly declarative and is expressed in myriad ways in today's society.

In contrast, submissive disciples like Enoch and Enos became ever more concerned for the welfare of others and led lives of very significant service (Moses 7:44; Enos 1:9, 13).

At judgment day it will not be possible to lodge any legitimate complaint against the justice of a God who allowed us to have the desires of our hearts, especially after His seeking to educate those desires through the teaching of His gospel truths—truths which can free us from the dark desires of selfishness.

> I ought not to harrow up in my desires, the firm decree of a just God, for I know that he granteth unto men according to their desire, whether it be unto death or unto life; yea, I know that he allotteth unto men, yea, decreeth unto them decrees which are unalterable, according to their wills, whether they be unto salvation or unto destruction (Alma 29:4).

> For I, the Lord, will judge all men according to their works, according to the desire of their hearts (D&C 137:9).

I the Lord search the heart, I try the reins, even to give every man according to his ways, and according to the fruit of his doings (Jeremiah 17:10).

It follows that refining our desires is a crucial first step on the path of submissiveness. The demands of discipleship should be our focus, not what we unsubmissively demand of God.

The demands disbelievers make of God would be comedy if they were not tragedy, some of those living in the Western Hemisphere before the birth of Jesus demanding, "Why will he not show himself in this land as well as in the land of Jerusalem?" (Helaman 16:19). Elsewhere some taunted Jesus while He hung on the cross, saying, "He saved others; let him save himself, if he be Christ" (Luke 23:35).

No divine demonstration followed these queries or taunts. The mortal desire for manifestations, but on our terms, is clearly inconsistent with the plan of the Lord. In times of stress He relies on the steadiness of our discipleship, not on an abundance of showmanship; on persuasion, not intimidation. As George MacDonald wrote of the nativity, "They all were looking for a king / To slay their foes and lift them high; / Thou cam'st, a little baby thing / That made a woman cry."[3]

When Jesus made His triumphal entry into Jerusalem, it was not with the glitter, pomp, and circumstance usual in such a situation: rather, he entered on the back of a foal (Matthew 21:5).

Jesus refused to perform a miracle for curious Herod (Luke 23:8). He praised John the Baptist as being a great prophet (Luke 7:28) even though the Baptist did no miracle

(John 10:41). The Master remained silent when Pilate asked Him to define truth (John 18:38). Earlier He could not do many mighty works in "his own country" because of the people's unbelief (Matthew 13:57–58). The Jews of that day clearly expected a Messiah who would rescue them politically; they did not understand that He had come to redeem them spiritually.

If the Lord were to show His power as some expect power to be used—which is virtually unthinkable—mortals would experience, among other things, prompt punishment rather than divine long-suffering. God would then stop all human suffering and silence all opposition to His work. In countless ways He would control the adverse effects of agency merely to prove that He was all-powerful. But He would not be all-loving, for in effect He would have derailed His plan of happiness! The enforced cooperation would not produce illuminated individuality but an indistinguishable "compound in one" (2 Nephi 2:11). We would then be back to that proposal of enforced "salvation" rejected so long ago (Moses 4:1).

Sometimes it is surprising that what is so obvious is so unseen, namely, that those who make demands of the Lord Himself (or His mortal leaders) to perform according to their criteria actually want a God who will serve them, not vice versa!

One great service performed by prophets is to state the obvious—unseen and unpopular though it may be.

If we truly follow Christ in our life's journey, we will share to some extent in His experiences, which can help us to become more like Him. When He says, "Come unto me," it is surely not accomplished in a single step, but each step is one step closer.

If we act aright for our true self-interest (2 Nephi 2:13–16), we are growing. If instead we are merely being "acted upon" by appetite and circumstance, we are docile, subordinating ourselves to stimuli which will drive us, oozing with self-pity, into the gulf of misery.

If instead of surrendering to Him we surrender to ourselves, we are surely bowing before an unjust and unwise emperor.

There can be no conditions attached to unconditional surrender to God. Unconditional surrender means we cannot keep our obsessions, possessions, or cheering constituencies. Even our customized security blankets must go.

Does this sound too severe and too sacrificing? If so, it is only until we realize that if we yield to Him, He will give us everything He has (D&C 84:38). Anyone, for example, who prepares to sit down at that culminating banquet with Jesus, Abraham, Isaac, and Jacob, certainly would not bring along his own beef jerky. Nor would he send an advance press agent to tout his accomplishments to that special company and in the presence of Him who trod the winepress alone (D&C 76:107).

Our personal trinkets, if carried even that far, are to be left outside at the doorstep or in the courtyard, where such clutter and debris would indicate the shedding of selfishness.

Some of us nevertheless feel as though we own ourselves, our time, our talents, and our possessions; these are signs of our self-sufficiency. Actually, God lends us breath and sustains us from moment to moment (Mosiah 2:21). Even our talents are gifts from Him. Whatever our possessions, these are merely on loan to us as accountable stewards. Possessions are not portable anyway. The submissive realize this.

Being too determined to receive recognition or credit indicates we are too concerned that others notice us. In such ego-centered circumstances others will surely "pass by" and, being preoccupied, we will "notice them not" (Mormon 8:39).

Our obsessions are as varied as our possessions. They may consist of a favored doctrinal emphasis, a favored Church program, or even a "trademark" leadership style. Having pride in these things, we sometimes polish them carefully and stand especially ready to defend them. Sometimes, if only unconsciously, we even cultivate a cheering and reinforcing constituency which, perhaps unintentionally, encourages us in our obsessions. To us, sooner or later, it will be said, "One thing thou lackest" (Mark 10:21). It is possible to have illegitimate pride in a legitimate role or in a deserved reputation. Such pride must go, for we are servants of Him who lived His unique life as a person of "no reputation" (Philippians 2:7).

Every obsession or preoccupation must give way in total submission. Only when we try to subdue our obsessions or preoccupations do we see how powerful they have become.

We have no evidence of Jesus' ever reflecting upon or discoursing immodestly upon His masterful performances, such as in the miracle of the loaves and fishes, in the raising of Lazarus, or in the healing of the ten lepers. He let his deeds speak for themselves, and He always attributed His power to the Father. Dare we do less as regards the much less we have achieved?

If we are spiritually submissive, not only is it a blessing unto us *per se* but also we are more easily heard and followed by the sincere. Any submissiveness and meekness on our part permits others to ponder our words or counsel. They need not first agonize over our motives or strip the bark of pride off any counsel. They are emancipated from such considerations. Genuine submissiveness removes such roadblocks to communication.

If we know who we are and whose we are, this belonging and acceptance results in much less need for mortal acceptance and acclaim. Indeed, the full giving of self—heart, mind, and strength—to Him leaves us with nothing else to give— no other "investments" to worry over. This is what the first great commandment is all about.

Unquestionably and demonstrably, the Lord uses our individual talents and gifts for the good of His work in serving others. However, the presence and usage of these talents and gifts does not relieve any of us of the obligation to achieve greater spiritual symmetry in our discipleship. The episode of the righteous man who lacked "one thing" is evidence of divine determination. If we take our discipleship as far as did that righteous man, even before that point, we must expect customized requirements to be made of us, hoping and praying all the while that we too do not go away "sorrowful" (Luke 18:23; Mark 10:22). At least he went away with "sorrowing," not in railing rejoinder to Jesus, "What a ridiculous requirement!" The divine direction had found its mark.

One of the most important contributions submissiveness makes to our individual happiness occurs in crucial moments of truth. These are moments when we teeter back and forth between surrender to Him and surrender to ourselves, between obedience and defiance. Submissiveness not only helps us to make right resolutions but also dissolves our pride, with its worry about what others will think if we admit error and yield to God.

We handle insightful feedback in many ways. We may deflect it deftly. We may ignore it stoically. We may accept it wholly or in part. Seldom, however, do we seek a helpful second or third opinion in such matters. Perhaps if there were multiple encouraging witnesses it might encourage us to change or to accept a particular challenge. Naaman found such help among his servants when he received a specialized direction (2 Kings 5:13).

The more serious the work on our own imperfections, the less we are judgmental of the imperfections in others. Meek Moroni's counsel is so appropriate: rather than condemn parents and predecessors for their imperfections, we can simply learn to be more wise than they have been (Mormon 9:31). There are more case studies available than studies of such cases.

Submissiveness to God enables us to govern ourselves, which is better than to "take a city" (Proverbs 16:32). Lacking this capacity we are vulnerable, like "a city which is broken down, and without walls" (Proverbs 25:28). We are vulnerable if we can be taken by a wave of emotion, invaded by an invidious impulse, roughed up by resentment, or engulfed by a surge of selfishness.

Submissiveness is admittedly and particularly hard to muster under certain conditions. For instance, if we think we own twenty-four hours a day, we can resent any unexpected imposition on our time, feeling we own the hour or the evening that is being "stolen" away from us.

In some of us there is such a deep need for comraderie and acceptance that, insincerely, we throw in with prevailing opinions or groups. We may think we are only setting aside a small principle for a small moment. But almost always it turns out to be much more.

While striving to walk the same straight and narrow path as other disciples, it is unwise for us to make comparisons. Peter questioned what John was to do. Jesus' rejoinder was, "What is that to thee? Follow thou me" (John 21:22). We mortals do not have all the data even on ourselves, let alone on others. But God does. Having faith in Him includes faith in His purposes not only for ourselves but also for others. Only He who carried the great cross can fully compare crosses.

The mother of James and John asked to have her sons sit later on Jesus' right and left hand. She was told, "Ye know not what ye ask" (Matthew 20:21). It had already been decided. She had asked amiss, as we all sometimes do (James 4:3; 2 Nephi 4:35; 3 Nephi 18:20; D&C 88:64–65). Sometimes we ask amiss because of our provincialism; this cannot be cured instantly, but we can trust submissively.

By putting everything we have on the altar of the Lord and not waiting for Him to give us a receipt, we show our submissiveness. Otherwise our giving may become linked with expecting recognition or with soliciting proof of the Lord's appreciation. After all, one day He will give everything to the faithful (D&C 84:38). God, who is perfect in His gratitude, "delights to honor those who serve" Him (D&C 76:5).

Mortal recognition is so fleeting, but God remembers always those who remember Him.

Even the conscientious need further refinement. Moses submitted to Jethro's directive counsel to delegate certain things to others, lest Moses wear away and the people wear away also (Exodus 18:18). Besides, Moses had more fundamental things to do: "And thou shalt teach them ordinances and laws, and shalt shew them the way wherein they must walk, and the work that they must do" (Exodus 18:20).

Similarly, George Washington experienced the refining process. His early frustrations and even failures provided highly relevant learning experiences well before he became the general of the Continental Army, or later a delegate to the 1787 Constitutional Convention, or, still later, the president of the United States. His past helped him succeed in his future because Washington was perceptive and meek:

> He was thus enrolled in a school of experience that would in many ways prepare him for the world-shaking task he was to undertake almost twenty years later. . . . Desertion was always to be a problem during Washington's military years. Now he learned in the most difficult of possible schools how to hold men by a combination of authority, violence, threats, persuasion, and inspiring leadership. . . .
>
> But Washington had not yet learned the unwisdom of attacking his civilian superiors for deficiencies beyond anyone's power to remedy. . . .

As his character and his world view expanded, more meanings became clear to him. He accurately defined his failures and worked out the reasons why he had failed. The results of this protracted self-education were to prove of the greatest importance to the creation of the United States.[4]

Had a younger Washington become proud or cynical, much of his later success could not have been achieved. Most of all, Washington learned, as so very few do, how to handle power, for he was an exception to the "almost all men" generalization (D&C 121:39).

In all history few men who possessed unassailable power have used that power so gently and self-effacingly for what their best instincts told them was the welfare of their neighbors and all mankind.[5]

God seeks to give us tutoring experiences so that, if we are submissive, we will have our own first-hand experiences to refer to in the eternities to come. We will have authentic, personal knowledge upon which to rely, not merely accurate abstractions. Since experiential learning is etched deeply into our souls, it is not easily forgotten.

Blessed, even so, are those of us who can trust God and be obedient without having to pass through each relevant learning experience. Yet each of us will end up with an impressive array of personal experiences as part of the luggage we take with us into the world to come. Not only can faith and patience be gained from those experiences, but so can the capacity to generalize wisely and humbly with an authority and authenticity which is everlasting.

Submission from experience is seen in the prodigal son's coming to a realization of his deplorable condition; he headed for home (Luke 15:20). Perchance did the prodigal, after wasting his inheritance, finally remember with humble appreciation his father's earlier generosity as the Holy Ghost preached to the prodigal from the pulpit of memory?

After the first refusal, Laman and Lemuel were reluctant to petition Laban further in the effort to obtain the brass plates. However, Nephi declared his determination: "As the Lord liveth, and as we live, we will not go down unto our father in the wilderness until we have accomplished the thing which the Lord hath commanded us" (1 Nephi 3:15).

Understandably, obedience to God is often equated with really hearing His word. "To really hear God's word inevitably involves one in an obedient response in action, prompted by faithfulness to and faith in the God who is revealing himself in and through particular historical events. Not to respond in obedient action is tantamount to unbelief." Hence the prophets sometimes chastise people for their blind eyes and deaf ears (Isaiah 6:9–10). "The inevitable consequence of failing to hear is rebellion or disobedience. . . . Rebellion is the sign that one has not really heard, since to hear implies a faith-obedience response."[6]

We are to hear with faith (Galatians 3:2). Hence the phrase from Paul, "faith comes by hearing, and hearing by the word of God" (Romans 10:17).

Little wonder then that, shut off from hearing the word, so many would end up living without God in the world.

Without Christ's help, reconciliation with God is something man could not achieve. Thus, man is estranged from God (Colossians 1:21), living "without God in the world" (Ephesians 2:12), "alienated from the life of God" (Ephesians 4:18). There are still others, of course, who are actually active enemies of God and hostile to His purposes (Romans 5:10; 8:7).

The Atonement was itself an act of reconciliation (2 Corinthians 5:19). Jesus "hath broken down the middle wall of partition between us . . . that he might reconcile [us] unto God" (Ephesians 2:14–16).

The theme of reconciliation is often found in the Book of Mormon as well: "Wherefore, my beloved brethren, reconcile yourselves to the will of God, and not to the will of the devil and the flesh; and remember, after ye are reconciled unto God, that it is only in and through the grace of God that ye are saved" (2 Nephi 10:24).

There is no such thing as one-party reconciliation. "And all things are of God, who hath reconciled us to himself by Jesus Christ, and hath given to us the ministry of reconciliation" (2 Corinthians 5:18). God stands ready to reconcile us to Him, waiting with open arms to receive us (Mormon 6:17). There is no such thing as a solo embrace.

When we are urged to put upon the altar of the Lord the sacrifice of a broken heart and a contrite spirit (Psalm 51:17; 3 Nephi 9:20), we are following the ancient counsel: "to obey is better than sacrifice, and to hearken than the fat of rams" (1 Samuel 15:22). Outward rituals can become near-empty ends in themselves. What we are actually placing on the altar to be consumed is the animal and carnal of our old selves. The need for that sacrifice has not been done away.

Spiritual submissiveness is not blind faith but deliberate obedience. It consists of proceeding on the basis of what we already know—proceeding to further subordination of the self within us. To begin to live with God in the world requires the expulsion of what is unacceptable in the old self—no minor adjustment. "Because the carnal mind is enmity against God: for it is not subject to the law of God, neither indeed can be" (Romans 8:7). "They are without God in the world, and they have gone contrary to the nature of God; therefore, they are in a state contrary to the nature of happiness" (Alma 41:11).

Sometimes we do not submit because we are preoccupied with the choking, consuming cares of the world. "And the cares of this world, and the deceitfulness of riches, and the lusts of other things entering in, choke the word, and it becometh unfruitful" (Mark 4:19; see also Luke 8:14; 21:34).

Being preoccupied with the cares of the world, we have no time for God and for spiritual things. This slackens the flow of divine data, since spiritual things are "*made known unto them according to their faith and repentance and their holy works*" (Alma 12:30, emphasis added). And again, "God . . . granteth unto men according to their desire, . . . he allotteth unto men, . . . according to their wills, whether they be unto salvation or unto destruction" (Alma 29:4).

Since God gives us revelations according to our desires, works, and worthiness, many mortals go on being ignorant of Him and estranged from His purposes, "without Christ, being aliens from the commonwealth of Israel, and strangers from the covenants of promise, having no hope, and without God in the world" (Ephesians 2:12; Mosiah 5:13).

More than in any other respect, it is in the requirement of spiritual submissiveness that the otherwise good individuals, whom the Lord describes as "honorable," consistently fall short. Honorable people may regard themselves as Christians—even as Latter-day Saints—but still not be valiant in their testimony of Jesus (D&C 76:79). The Prophet Joseph Smith said: "And man may believe that Jesus Christ is the Son of God, and be happy in that belief, and yet not obey his commandments, and at last be cut down for disobedience to the Lord's righteous requirements."[7]

One can see why it so happens. Commitment can be less than complete, as in the case of the righteous young man who could not bear the customized commandment he received from Jesus (Matthew 19:21–22).

A striking initial difference in the degree of submissiveness is seen between two military men: Naaman, the Syrian commander, and the Roman centurion. Naaman resented the fact that the prophet would not even come out of his house to talk to him, but instead sent instructions (2 Kings 5:9–12). The centurion did not even ask for Jesus to come to his ailing servant, but merely said, "Speak the word only, and my servant shall be healed" (Matthew 8:5–13).

The fashions of the world do clearly devalue submissiveness to God and do exclude the spiritual. Yet surely "the fashion of this world passeth away" (1 Corinthians 7:31). The ways of the world tend to reinforce some people's conclusion that "this is all there is, so make the most of it." Soon, however, the consequences of hedonism will give rise to

old-fashioned fear in the hearts of many people. The cocksure-
ness will give away to distress:

> I have . . . decreed wars upon the face of the earth,
> and the wicked shall slay the wicked, and fear shall come
> upon every man (D&C 63:33).

> And all things shall be in commotion; and surely,
> men's hearts shall fail them; for fear shall come upon all
> people (D&C 88:91).

Meanwhile, the proud and some honorable people will
"walk in their own ways" and seek to establish their own substitute forms of righteousness:

> They seek not the Lord to establish his righ-
> teousness, but every man walketh in his own way, and
> after the image of his own god, whose image is in the
> likeness of the world, and whose substance is that of an
> idol, which waxeth old and shall perish in Babylon, even
> Babylon the great, which shall fall (D&C 1:16).

These things happen because they, "being ignorant of
God's righteousness, and going about to establish their own
righteousness, have not submitted themselves unto the righteousness of God" (Romans 10:3).

Only such sweeping perspective as comes from seers can
save us from ourselves (Mosiah 8:17).

One of the obvious challenges occurs because the Lord
has delegated some of His authority for developmental purposes. It is His authority, but we who use it are not yet sufficiently like Him to unfailingly use it as we should. Anciently

the Lord counseled that people were to be careful in ruling over others; they were not to do it "with rigour" (Leviticus 25:43, 46, 53). In the Moffatt translation of the Bible the phrase is translated, "you must not lord it over him harshly, but stand in awe of your God." The leadership style which befits the use of God's authority is to be found in the revelation given to Joseph Smith in Liberty Jail (D&C 121).

Regardless of the leadership style, there are some who simply do not want anyone to rule over them at all, however justly and meekly. It happened early in Moses' ministry:

> For he [Moses] supposed his brethren would have understood how that God by his hand would deliver them: but they understood not.
>
> And the next day he shewed himself unto them as they strove, and would have set them at one again, saying, Sirs, ye are brethren; why do ye wrong one to another?
>
> But he that did his neighbour wrong thrust him away, saying, Who made thee a ruler and a judge over us? (Acts 7:25–27).

> And they gathered themselves together against Moses and against Aaron, and said unto them, Ye take too much upon you, seeing all the congregation are holy, every one of them, and the Lord is among them: wherefore then lift ye up yourselves above the congregation of the Lord? . . .
>
> Is it a small thing that . . . thou make thyself altogether a prince over us? (Numbers 16:3, 13).

> And they said, Hath the Lord indeed spoken only by Moses? hath he not spoken also by us? And the Lord heard it.
>
> (Now the man Moses was very meek, above all the men which were upon the face of the earth) (Numbers 12:2–3).

The paranoia can be compelling:

> Our brother Nephi, . . . has taken it upon him to be our ruler and our teacher, who are his elder brethren.
>
> Now, he says that the Lord has talked with him, and also that angels have ministered unto him. But behold, we know that he lies unto us; . . . thinking, perhaps, that he may lead us away into some strange wilderness; and after he has led us away, he has thought to make himself a king and a ruler over us, that he may do with us according to his will and pleasure (1 Nephi 16:37–38).

> Yea, they did murmur against me, saying: Our younger brother thinks to rule over us; . . . For behold, we will not have him to be our ruler; for it belongs unto us, who are the elder brethren, to rule over this people. (2 Nephi 5:3).

Paul's counsel to submit was given in order to have gladness instead of sadness: "Obey them that have the rule over you, and submit yourselves; for they watch for your souls, as they that must give account, that they may do it with joy, and not with grief" (Hebrews 13:17).

Submitting to the leadership, counsel, and direction of those placed over us may test us, particularly in view of the imperfections leaders have. Frequently, though, the test shows up the imperfections of the one being led. A most interesting example occurs in the case of an early member of the Church, Simonds Ryder. This man had been a member of the Campbellite movement and was among those from that movement who joined the Church in 1831. Because his name was misspelled in a revelation calling him on a mission, he began to be disillusioned and finally he apostatized. In 1832, he helped tar and feather Joseph Smith.[8] From member to mobocrat in a matter of months!

In the course of the Church's history in this dispensation others have managed to become offended by one thing or another. Often the offense occurred because of doctrines with which they were not in full accord, or because they were not given the recognition to which they thought they were entitled. What has happened in this dispensation in this respect likely mirrors what has happened in other dispensations.

It is often a matter of pride as to whose agendum comes first. What those who are proud, having "not submitted themselves unto the righteousness of God" (Romans 10:3), are determined to do is sometimes not actually inappropriate and may even involve doing good. The problem lies in their excluding that which God or his leaders counsel them to do. Pressing one's own agendum to the exclusion of divine counsel (whether the latter is given by the Spirit, the scriptures, or those in authority over us) puts us in spiritual jeopardy. If we are submissive, we will demonstrate "unfeigned love of the brethren" (1 Peter 1:22).

After all, as Alma said, discipleship means being "led by

the Holy Spirit, becoming humble, meek, submissive, patient, full of love, and all long-suffering" (Alma 13:28). Moreover, the companion plea is that "ye should be humble, and be submissive and gentle; easy to be entreated; full of patience and long-suffering; being temperate in all things" (Alma 7:23). Being easy to be entreated requires intellectual humility. This is at obvious odds with the styles and panache of the world.

Jesus, in his great high priestly prayer, said, "This is life eternal, that they might know thee the only true God, and Jesus Christ, whom thou hast sent" (John 17:3). Knowing the Lord is more than simply acknowledging that He is there. Knowing Him includes understanding His purposes and allowing for His tutorial activism as it affects us and those we love.

If we obey God, we will have the Holy Ghost to be with us, "whom God hath given to them that obey Him" (Acts 5:32).

It was Jesus' full obedience that fully ransomed us all: "So by the obedience of one shall many be made righteous" (Romans 5:19). Marvelous as Jesus was, "though he were a son, yet learned he obedience by the things which he suffered." Thereby Jesus was made perfect (Hebrews 5:8–9). One wonders how much Jesus actually needed to learn by way of obedience. Having been so obedient and preeminent premortally, perhaps He needed only to provide a mortal verification of His obedience already so well established. Then it would be clearly "on the record," underscoring the justice of God as "no respecter of persons" (Romans 2:11).

Spiritual submissiveness widens and extends our vision of the most fundamental things, such as how we see life, ourselves, and our circumstances. Mind, thought, and intellect then turns to Jesus, "bringing into captivity every thought to the obedience of Christ" (2 Corinthians 10:5). Then we will also go the second mile, just as Paul assuringly wrote to a colleague, "knowing that thou wilt also do more than I say" (Philemon 1:21). Others "have not learned to be obedient to the things which I required at their hands" (D&C 105:3).

Are we willing to become humble because of the word? Or will our humility depend solely upon the circumstance (Alma 32:13–16)?

How important the plates of brass were! Among many things, they testified that "a man must be obedient to the commandments of God. . . . Wherefore, if ye shall be obedient to the commandments, and endure to the end, ye shall be saved at the last day" (1 Nephi 22:30–31). Being willing to follow the commandments is no small task, depending upon our being "obedient unto the Lord" and his prophets and scriptures: "For behold, as yet, ye have been obedient unto the word of the Lord, which I have given unto you" (Jacob 2:4). And Joseph Smith said: "But when [a person] consents to obey the Gospel, whether here or in the world of spirits, he is saved. . . . All will suffer until they obey Christ himself."[9]

The Abraham/Isaac sacrifice episode, a similitude of God's giving His Only Begotten Son in the Atonement (Jacob 4:5), is full of implications which we cannot now fully measure. Abraham was willing to offer his son Isaac. Hence the similitude also shows a yielding Father-God as well as a willing Son. The implications are profound indeed!

After King Benjamin's great sermon the assembled congregation said they were willing "to be obedient to [God's] commandments in all things that he shall command us, all the remainder of our days." By the gift of discernment the king knew of their changed condition: "Your hearts are changed through faith in his name," he said, noting that they had taken upon them "the name of Christ, all you that have entered into the covenant with God that ye should be obedient unto the end of your lives" (Mosiah 5:5–8).

With greater knowledge, however, come greater risks, as Joseph Smith pointed out:

> There is a superior intelligence bestowed upon such as obey the Gospel with full purpose of heart, which, if sinned against, the apostate is left naked and destitute of the Spirit of God, and he is, in truth, nigh unto cursing, and his end is to be burned. When once that light which was in them is taken from them, they become as much darkened as they were previously enlightened, and then, no marvel, if all their power should be enlisted against the truth, and they, Judas like, seek the destruction of those who were their greatest benefactors.[10]

Thus we see how important it is for us both to submit and then also to endure well to the end. It is a rigorous combination that leaves no room for sloppiness. So much depends upon parents and teachers: "Yea, and they did obey and observe to perform every word of command with exactness; yea, and even according to their faith it was done unto them; and I did remember the words which they said unto me that their mothers had taught them" (Alma 57:21).

If we are submissive, we will not be as easily offended. Jesus was not offended because of the wrongs done to Him, rather, He was worried over the offender. He could look upon offenses caused by others as reflecting deficiencies or earlier wounds in their lives. If they would yield to Him, Jesus could heal all these (3 Nephi 18:32). Otherwise, healing scabs are sometimes torn off by fresh offenses, bringing needless, repetitive pain.

Tough or tutorial love requires not only much of us but also considerable courage on the part of those who teach us. Tutorial love involves real caring, with the capacity to customize challenges—just as God does.

The most striking example of tutorial love is that which the Only Begotten Son experienced in carrying out the plans of His perfect Father. Jesus, who had served the best of all, experienced the worst of all. The only sin-free soul suffered the sins of all.

Examples of directing and tutorial love follow, illustrating yet another side of submissiveness.

President Gordon B. Hinckley has written about his early and discouraging days as a missionary in England.

> I was not well when I arrived. Those first few weeks, because of illness and the opposition which we felt, I was discouraged. I wrote a letter home to my good father and said that I felt I was wasting my time and his money. He was my father and my stake president, and he was a wise and inspired man. He wrote a very short letter to me which said, "Dear Gordon, I have your recent letter. I have only one suggestion: forget yourself and go to work." Earlier that morning in our scripture class my companion and I had read these words of the

Lord: "Whosoever will save his life shall lose it; but whosoever shall lose his life for my sake and the gospel's, the same shall save it" (Mark 8:35).

Those words of the Master, followed by my father's letter with his counsel to forget myself and go to work, went into my very being. With my father's letter in hand, I went into our bedroom in the house at 15 Wadham Road, where we lived, and got on my knees and made a pledge with the Lord. I covenanted that I would try to forget myself and lose myself in His service.[11]

President Thomas S. Monson has shared this illuminating illustration with us:

> While serving in Guatemala as a missionary for The Church of Jesus Christ of Latter-day Saints, Randall Ellsworth survived a devastating earthquake that hurled a beam down on his back, paralyzing his legs and severely damaging his kidneys. He was the only American injured in the quake, which claimed the lives of some eighteen thousand persons.
>
> On his return to Guatemala, Randall Ellsworth supported himself with the help of two canes. His walk was slow and deliberate. Then one day, as he stood before his mission president, Elder Ellsworth heard these almost unbelievable words spoken: "You have been the recipient of a miracle," said the mission president. "Your faith has been rewarded. If you have the necessary confidence, if you have abiding faith, if you have supreme courage, place those two canes on my desk and walk."
>
> After a long pause, first one cane and then the other

was placed on the desk, and a missionary walked. It was halting, it was painful—but he walked, never again to need the canes.[12]

Elder Spencer W. Kimball, after his throat surgery, experienced some tutorial love at the hands of a loving colleague, Elder Harold B. Lee:

> At the Houston conference Elder Lee, the senior of the two apostles, announced Elder Kimball as the next speaker. He stood, opened his mouth, but only an ugly grating noise came out. He swallowed and gulped and tried again, with the same sickening feeling. The thought came: "Better quit—you can't do it—you can't impose on the people like this." But he tried again, this time found his voice, and delivered his short sermon. Then he turned to Elder Lee, shrugged helplessly and sat down. Elder Lee put his hand on him and said, "Thank you, Brother Kimball."
>
> The next day there was another meeting in Houston. Elder Lee, in charge, announced Elder Kimball as the next speaker. He stood and "made the most terrible sound you can imagine" until finally he found his voice and gave his sermon. Then he sat down, buried his head in his hands and mourned. "I was crying gallons of tears inside. I don't think they showed. But I really thought I was through, that I'd never preach again, that I wouldn't even try."
>
> Three days later, driving by car to Texarkana, he passed Elder Lee a note: "I hope you won't embarrass me again." Elder Lee jovially responded, "Oh, I'm sure

we'll call on you again. I think it's important for the people to hear your witness." Elder Kimball answered nothing. He knew he would do anything Elder Lee, his senior, asked. But inside he rebelled at the thought.

The conference at Texarkana was held in a long, narrow Methodist chapel. True to his word, Elder Lee called on his companion apostle to speak. It seemed impossible. The public address system was out. The chapel was huge. Outside the window was the highway, with trucks climbing a hill, grinding and shifting gears. Elder Kimball stood and began, "Brothers and Sisters . . ." He prayed silently, he strained, the words came. For ten minutes he bore his testimony. Every person in the chapel heard him. He sat down and Elder Lee put his arm around him and said, "That's right, Spencer."[13]

Blessed is he or she who is so loved as to be tutored!

No wonder sainthood centers on such submissiveness. We become saintly only when, among other things, we are "willing to submit to all things whatsoever the Lord seeth fit to inflict upon [us], even as a child doth submit to his father" (Mosiah 3:19).

Yet after initial submission what endurance is required!

7

"If Thou Endure Well"

The ever more rapid passing of time tends to provide a much keener appreciation for those disciples who "endure well" (D&C 121:8) to the end. However, this sobering challenge is not just for the aging.

To "endure well" to the end is actually enduring well to the very beginning. Meanwhile, this life is the second estate over the prospects of which we once shouted for joy (Job 38:7), even though there may be brief moments when we might wonder what all that shouting was about.

But here we are in the midst of "all these things," including those things which the tutoring Lord "seeth fit to inflict upon us" (Mosiah 3:19; 1 Peter 4:19). Can we be like a group of ancient American Saints who experienced some special stress and strain? They carried some unusual burdens, but the scriptures say "they did submit cheerfully and with patience to all the will of the Lord" (Mosiah 24:15). Our capacity to love and to endure well are bound together by patience.

Real faith in God includes faith in His timing. God did not, for instance, rush the Restoration, which required, among other things, adequate political and religious freedom. To have rushed would have been to crush human agency or to risk failure because of premature action. Instead, God's plan of mercy provides, as we know, for those who lived in the darkness of pre-Restoration days, as well as for all others who had no opportunity to receive the gospel in mortality.

God's waiting for our readiness continues even now, for "the Lord is not slack concerning his promise, as some men count slackness; but is longsuffering to us-ward, not willing that any should perish, but that all should come to repentance" (2 Peter 3:9).

As are all the Christian virtues, endurance is talked about and written of both trenchantly and humorously, both scripturally and otherwise:

Shakespeare wrote:

For there was never yet philosopher
that could endure the toothache patiently.

La Rochefoucauld said:

We all have strength enough to endure the misfortunes of others.

William Walsh observed:

I can endure my own despair,
But not another's hope.

Emerson asserted:

Some of your hurts you have cured,
And the sharpest you still have survived,

But what torments of grief you endured
From evils which never arrived!

Yeats spoke of enduring:

Endure that toil of growing up;
The ignominy of boyhood; the distress
Of boyhood changing into man;
The unfinished man and his pain.[1]

More to the point are key scriptures pertaining to this crowning quality:

> And now, my beloved brethren, I know by this that unless a man shall endure to the end, *in following the example of the Son of the living God,* he cannot be saved. . . .
>
> Wherefore, ye must *press forward with a steadfastness* in Christ, having a *perfect brightness of hope,* and a *love of God* and *of all* men. Wherefore, if ye shall press forward, *feasting upon* the *word of Christ,* and *endure to the end,* behold, thus saith the Father: Ye shall have eternal life (2 Nephi 31:16, 20; emphasis added).

Hence we are not merely to exist to the end. Rather, we are to persist "in following the example of the Son of the living God." That's quite a different emphasis from what we sometimes think of in connection with enduring! No wonder, then, that Philip James Bailey wrote:

There is no disappointment we endure
One half so great as that we are to ourselves.[2]

Especially it may be so for Latter-day Saints, who have great expectations and then must endure the difference between what we could be and what we are, all the while trying to make use of the divine discontent within us.

Our emphasis, therefore, should be on "doing" and "becoming," not just on surviving; on serving others, not just serving time.

Thus this quality of graceful endurance includes, but is more than, hanging on "for one moment more." Passing beyond breaking points without breaking takes the form of endurance.

Besides, this life is not really chronological but experiential. Quoting Philip James Bailey again:

> We live in deeds, not years; in thoughts, not breaths;
> In feelings, not in figures on a dial.
> We should count time by heart-throbs.[3]

Salient scriptures, each to be savored in its particular evocativeness, describe the many dimensions of endurance:

> Blessed is the man that endureth temptation: for when he is tried, he shall receive the crown of life, which the Lord hath promised to them that love him (James 1:12).

Paul promised us either a way to escape or help to bear temptation, meaning affliction too:

> God is faithful, who will not suffer you to be tempted above that ye are able; but will with the temptation also

make a way to escape, that ye may be able to bear it (1 Corinthians 10:13).

Can we endure hatred, misrepresentation, and misunderstanding?

And ye shall be hated of all men for my name's sake: but he that endureth to the end shall be saved (Matthew 10:22).

Misunderstanding goes with this telestial territory. Moreover, enduring well involves all of life's seasons, not just one:

And [they] have no root in themselves, and so endure *but for a time:* afterward, when affliction or persecution ariseth for the word's sake, immediately they are offended (Mark 4:17, emphasis added).

And now, my son, I trust that I shall have great joy in you, because of your steadiness and your faithfulness unto God; for as you have commenced in your youth to look to the Lord your God, even so I hope that you will continue in keeping his commandments; for blessed is he that endureth to the end (Alma 38:2).

The requirement to endure well is not optional.

And again, I would that ye should learn that he only is saved who endureth unto the end (D&C 53:7).

The quality being focused on includes intellectual as well as behavioral endurance:

For the time will come when they will not endure
sound doctrine (2 Timothy 4:3).

Can we endure the hard doctrines and truths? Or will we
be like those who could not handle Jesus' hard sayings?

From that time many of his disciples went back,
and walked no more with him (John 6:66).

In a world of shifting values we can scarcely "hold fast"
except we "hold fast" to the word of God:

And I said unto them that . . . whoso would
hearken unto the word of God, and would hold fast
unto it, they would never perish; neither could the
temptations and the fiery darts of the adversary overpower them (1 Nephi 15:24).

The promises are magnificent for those who do "endure
well":

Look unto me, and endure to the end, and ye shall
live; for unto him that endureth to the end will I give
eternal life (3 Nephi 15:9).

And blessed are they who shall seek to bring forth
my Zion at that day, for they shall have the gift and the
power of the Holy Ghost; and if they endure unto the
end they shall be lifted up at the last day, and shall be
saved in the everlasting kingdom of the Lamb (1 Nephi
13:37).

And if you keep my commandments and endure to

the end you shall have eternal life, which gift is the greatest of all the gifts of God (D&C 14:7).

Nevertheless, he that endureth in faith and doeth my will, the same shall overcome, and shall receive an inheritance upon the earth when the day of transfiguration shall come (D&C 63:20).

But the sequence is clear: promises are kept only *after* performance is actualized:

And so, *after he had patiently endured*, he obtained the promise (Hebrews 6:15, emphasis added).

Nor are we to misread God's tutoring love, for He would not be a loving Father if He ignored our imperfections:

If ye endure chastening, God dealeth with you as with sons; for what son is he whom the father chasteneth not (Hebrews 12:7)?

For all those who will not endure chastening, *but deny me,* cannot be sanctified (D&C 101:5, emphasis added).

Why is nonendurance a denial of the Lord? Because giving up is a denial of the immense potential of our spirit birth and of the Lord's loving capacity to see us through "all these things."

We should see life, therefore, as being comprised of clusters of soul-stretching experiences, even when these are overlain by seeming ordinariness or are plainly wrapped in routine. Thus some who are chronologically very young can be Methuselahs as to their maturity in spiritual things.

So much of life's curriculum, therefore, consists of efforts by the Lord to get and keep our attention. Ironically, the stimuli He uses are often that which is seen by us as something to endure. Sometimes what we are actually being asked to endure is His "help": help to draw us away from the cares of the world; help to draw us away from self-centeredness; attention-getting help when we have ignored the still, small voice; help in the shaping of our souls; and help to keep promises we made so long ago. In some instances the stimuli can be severe and sharp: "And thus we see that except the Lord doth chasten his people with many afflictions, yea, except he doth visit them with death and with terror, and with famine and with all manner of pestilence, they will not remember him" (Helaman 12:3).

There is clearly no immunity from such stimuli or other afflictions, whether of the self-induced variety or the divine-tutorial type. Either way, however, the Lord can help us so that our afflictions can be "swallowed up in the joy of Christ" (Alma 31:38). The sour notes are lost amid a symphony of salvational sounds.

Paul said he died "daily" (1 Corinthians 15:31). Such is the process of putting off the old self as one becomes a man or woman of Christ. In this task, quick-change artists are rare.

Interacting in this mortal world with so many others, as we do, we constitute each other's clinical material, agency and all! This means enduring each other's immaturity—which, compounded, produces considerable perplexity. As to what is happening inexplicably to us and around us, we can say: "I know that [God] loveth his children; nevertheless, I do not know the meaning of all things" (1 Nephi 11:17).

There have been and will be times in each of our lives when such faith must be the bottom line: We don't know what is happening to us or around us, but we know that God loves us, and knowing that, for the moment, is enough.

We have some marvelous models on enduring uncertainty and on trusting God.

First, there were the three young men, Shadrach, Meshach, and Abed-nego, whose response to a persecuting king was, as they were about to be thrown into a fiery furnace heated seven times its usual capacity:

> If it be so, our God whom we serve is able to deliver us from the burning fiery furnace . . .

And then the three words:

> But if not, be it known unto thee, O king, that we will not serve thy gods, nor worship the golden image which thou hast set up (Daniel 3:17–18, emphasis added).

But if not . . . There will be times in each of our lives when our faith must not be conditioned upon God's rescuing or relieving us, because in fact He may not—at least, not as we would choose to be rescued.

Second, matching those three young men are three young women whose names we do not have. They are mentioned in the book of Abraham, remarkable young women about whom I am anxious to know more. They were actually sacrificed upon the altar because "they would not bow down to worship [an idol] of wood or stone" (Abraham 1:11). Some day the faithful will get to meet them.

A third example is remarkable Mary, the mother of Jesus. The record of when she was confronted with the great announcement contains an interesting set of words. In response to the angel's amazing statement, Mary was perplexed about what lay ahead, and the birth of the Son of God through her: "And Mary said, Behold the handmaid of the Lord; be it unto me according to thy word. And the angel departed from her" (Luke 1:38).

"But if not . . ." "Be it unto me according to thy word." These are most compressed expressions of the capacity to endure.

Enduring is, quite naturally, equated in some respects with holding out or holding fast. It certainly includes the capacity to endure for one moment more. It also includes, as we have noted, enduring customized tests of our trust in God. A Nephite prophet had angered corrupt judges by denouncing them and, by inspiration, advised them of the murder of a judge and the murderer's identity. Surely he knew that by so declaring he could be entrapped and accused of being a "confederate" in the crime—which indeed happened. Then further inspiration came by which the murderer was caused to confess the crime. Had Nephi been disobedient or lacking in faith or endurance, the harvest of souls who came to believe him at that time would not have occurred (Helaman 8:27–9:41).

This capacity to endure well permits us, when required, to "be still and know that [he is] God," for "the Lord of hosts is with us" (Psalm 46:10, 11). At other times, we are to "stand still," as did the children of Israel at the edge of an intimidating and, as yet, unparted Red Sea. "The Lord shall fight for you, and ye shall hold your peace" (Exodus 14:13–14).

We will never see the spiritual scenery beyond the next ridge unless we press forward on the strait and narrow path. Peter, being tough minded as well as loving, made the test of our patience even more precise and demanding when he said: "For what glory is it, if, when ye be buffeted for your faults, ye shall take it patiently? but if, when ye do well, and suffer for it, ye take it patiently, this is acceptable with God" (1 Peter 2:20).

In our dispensation we have been advised: "My people must be tried in all things, that they may be prepared to receive the glory that I have for them, even the glory of Zion; and he that will not bear chastisement is not worthy of my kingdom" (D&C 136:31).

The dues of durable discipleship are high indeed. Yet how much we can *take* so often determines how much we can then *give*.

Learning to "endure well" is being able to lose face without losing heart. It is being able to pass through seeming or real injustice, as did Job, without "charging God foolishly" (Job 1:22).

The Christian virtues are those very qualities which will rise with us in the resurrection. To the degree that we have developed them in this world, we will have so much the advantage in the world to come (D&C 130:19). Endurance is the porter, bearing other qualities forward.

Our spiritual development is to be achieved amid differentially dispensed measures of time. For some of the unwell and aged, unwanted time can be like taffy to be shaken free of. Others are required to endure the sudden karate chop of changed circumstances.

Even so, time is relative, and these things "shall be but a small moment" (D&C 121:7). "For our light affliction, which is but for a moment, worketh for us a far more exceeding and eternal weight of glory" (2 Corinthians 4:17).

Meanwhile, if we will do as invited, our load will be lightened by "casting all your care upon him; for he careth for you" (1 Peter 5:7).

It is easier to endure without resentment if we remember how and why this life is so structured: "For it must needs be, that there is an opposition in all things. If not so . . . righteousness could not be brought to pass" (2 Nephi 2:11). But it is all metered out to us in terms of our bearing capacity (D&C 50:40).

This opposition includes the stern and demanding isometrics of being pitted against our old selves. It is the sternest, most persistent competition we shall know, especially in view of the fact that Satan uses our old selves as his surrogates. It is in this competition especially that we must "come off conquerer" (D&C 10:5; Moroni 9:6; 1 Nephi 22:26).

Enduring also includes the in-between periods of life. Winston Churchill endured a decade (1929–39) of what were called his "wilderness years." He was outside the circles of power, his talents being largely unused though his accurate warning voice was raised. Many assumed his political career to be over. But his time came in his country's hour of need, and his enduring had not been in vain.

Thackeray wrote superbly of those circumstances in which "to endure is greater than to dare; to tire out hostile fortune; to be daunted by no difficulty; to keep heart when all have lost it; to go through intrigue spotless; to forego even ambition when the end is gained—who can say this is not greatness?"[4]

Though we can endure being abused, can we endure being *underwhelmed, unused,* and *unsung*? Can we endure almost uninterrupted unresponsiveness?

The prophet Ether endured a time in which he preached the gospel from "the morning, even to the going down of the sun" but went unheeded (Ether 12:3).

As commanded, Mormon even endured the unusual circumstance of being an "idle witness" in order to manifest certain things to the world (Mormon 3:16).

Whether the test is illness, pain, deprivation, or being passed over, being ignored, being underwhelmed, or working one's way through doubts, what are to be sustained are trust and faith in God *and* in His plan—including in His timing.

Sustained discipleship includes resisting, and chopping back again and again, the encroaching crabgrass cares of the world. These cares, along with temptation, persecution, and tribulation, are what usually cause us to slacken and give up.

Thus with increasing understanding we see that, while enduring is more than simply waiting, it includes waiting. But even waiting can be used to facilitate our becoming more like Jesus. Therefore, we should be "anxiously engaged," even when it seems to us we are doing no more than waiting. Thus we can be about our Father's business even when it seems for the moment that we are overcome by ordinariness and routine. Our enduring is easier if we see it as a part of God's unfolding.

Besides, we were never promised precision in this life. Nor should the gospel be expected to lend itself to glib mortal explanations in all circumstances—it is too divinely comprehensive for that. We endure even when we cannot explain, and it is silence that bespeaks certitude.

With the gift of agency to mankind, life cannot possibly present a perfectly tidy picture. The ambiguities of circumstances are partly, if not largely, the cumulative result of our varied use of our moral agency, but also of the structure of life itself.

But some will ask, what of those circumstances when individuals appear to be no more than a surviving vegetable, unable to express themselves, not able to serve? We are not equipped to answer fully such questions. We should not assume, however, that just because something is unexplainable by us it is unexplainable. Meanwhile we see in such a situation opportunities for service, even when the one being served may not know of the service.

There are also the flat periods in life which may well be the periods during which—before new lessons come—the past lessons of life are allowed to seep, quietly and deeply, into the marrow of the soul.

Those outwardly flat periods, when enduring well may not seem very purposeful, are probably the times when needed attitudinal alignments are quietly occurring. Trying to observe the slow shift from self-centeredness to empathy is like trying to watch grass grow. An experience is thus not only endured but also absorbed and perused, almost unconsciously, for its value. Such a process takes time. Therefore it is we, not God, who need more time. This fact should give us pause in our prayers when we would hasten the day even as, for others, God must hold back the dawn.

This whole process is one which can scarcely be rushed—anymore than one can rush through the period of one's youth in order to be done with acne and low teenage self-esteem.

It is the love, mercy, and justice of God which can cause Him to wait long-sufferingly. Remember the search for a handful of righteous individuals who, if found, would have caused God to spare Sodom and Gomorrah. One cannot help but muse over the question of which few of Sodom's citizens—given a little more reforming effort—had the best chance to make up the critical mass of ten and thereby save a city. God waited, but the ten could not be found.

Our premortal choices were made earlier. Our consent was given—in the first estate—concerning our second estate. This being so, enduring well becomes not only a prime quality but also a reasonable requirement. It calls for shoulder squaring and not shoulder shrugging, and for realizing, as a wise C. S. Lewis wrote, that the "cross comes before the crown, and tomorrow is a Monday morning."[5]

Meanwhile, mortality involves teeth to be brushed, beds to be made, cars to be repaired, diapers to be changed, groceries to be bought—such an endless array of mundane matters. In the midst of these, however, is the real business of living—a friendship to be formed, a marriage to be mended, a child to be encouraged, a truth to be driven home, an apology to be made, a Christian attribute to be further developed.

Finally, not all of us die quietly of heart attacks in our sleep at an advanced age. Nor can we always use our faith and prayers to block all the exit doors from mortality, all the time, for all the people. It is as important that there be ways out of this mortal schoolhouse as that there be ways in. There must be endings even for graceful enduring.

Whether life is long or short, the Apostle John summed it up so well: "Here is the patience of the saints: here are they that keep the commandments of God, and the faith of Jesus" (Revelation 14:12).

It is possible to know when, at least basically, we please God. In fact, Joseph Smith taught that one of the conditions of genuine faith is to have "an actual knowledge that the course of life which [one] is pursuing is according to [God's] will."[6] We observe that, writing about Enoch, Paul noted that "before his translation he had this testimony, that he pleased God" (Hebrews 11:5). The Prophet and his associates went further, saying that unless people have such an assurance, "they will grow weary in their minds, and faint."[7] This is the same concern Paul addressed in his epistle to the Hebrews (Hebrews 12:1–3). Significantly, Paul urged members to jettison—"lay aside"—the wearying baggage of sin and to look to Jesus as their example, "lest ye be wearied and faint in your minds."

There are some among us who have become intellectually weary and who faint in their minds because they are malnourished; they are not partaking regularly of the fulness of the gospel feast. Partaking of that feast in the appropriate spiritual rhythm leads to what Amulek described as giving "thanksgiving daily." Then we can "take up the cross daily," and then "endure in faith on his name to the end" (Alma 34:38; Luke 9:23; D&C 20:29).

Spiritual staying power requires strength—strength to be achieved by feasting upon the gospel of Jesus Christ regularly, deeply, and perceptively. If we go unnourished by the gospel feast which God has generously spread before us, we will be vulnerable instead of durable.

Our basic course can be correct, then, even as we continue to work diligently on our deficiencies, for the committed know "what manner of persons" we "ought . . . to be" (2 Peter 3:11; 3 Nephi 27:27). Once we have taken his yoke upon us, we will learn of him (Matthew 11:29) and learn to be more like Him. Some "rest unto your souls" can come even amid that labor, flowing from the assurance noted above.

Consider, on the other hand, those who do not know God or His purposes, or understand His attributes—both conditions of real faith. A vague belief in God will not produce staying power, nor will a faint understanding of life's purposes help us to carry our cross.

Similarly, fair weather followership cannot see us through life's stormy seasons. Instead, such will "faint in [their] minds" and grow weary. Surely what some commentators have called "a weariness in the west," referring to western civilization, reflects western civilization's increasing secularization!

There is a difference between stumbling along the pathway to perfection even as we display our humanness, and wandering about aimlessly in a desert of despair and disbelief.

The more we become like Christ, the closer we will come to Him and the more we will trust Him. Submission, after all, is the ultimate adoration. To the submissive who frequent His holy temples will He impart more of "the mysteries of the kingdom."

8

"The Mysteries of the Kingdom"

The word *mystery,* as used in scriptures, may refer to certain truths and doctrines. Instead of being complex or profound, though, as the word might sometimes connote, such truths are usually very simple. In fact they are so simple as to be rejected and scorned by some, which may be a reason for divine restraint in imparting them. Jacob, for instance, used the word *mystery* to refer to the scattering of Israel, which he explained in the allegory of the tame and wild olive trees: "Behold, my beloved brethren, I will unfold this mystery unto you; if I do not, by any means, get shaken from my firmness in the Spirit, and stumble because of my over anxiety for you" (Jacob 4:18).

Alma, in instructing his son Corianton, unfolded a "mystery" concerning the resurrection of the dead (Alma 40:3). And King Benjamin, talking to his sons, expressed appreciation that the Nephites had the brass plates scriptures, "that we might read and understand of [God's] mysteries, and have his commandments always before our eyes" (Mosiah 1:5).

Sometimes, however, the use of the term involves the holy temples. The Lord said, "Therefore, I will unfold unto them this great mystery" (D&C 10:64), and in the succeeding verse, the hen gathering her chickens, according to the Prophet Joseph Smith, refers to the desire of the Lord to gather his people in his holy temples.[1]

> A large assembly of Saints met at the Temple & were addressed by President Joseph Smith He took for the foundation of his discourse the words of Jesus to the *Jews* how oft would I have gatherd you togetherd as a hen gathereth her chickens under wings. . . . The main object was to build unto the Lord an house whereby he could reveal unto his people the ordinances of his house and glories of his kingdom & teach the peopl the ways of salvation for their are certain ordinances & principles that when they are taught and practized, must be done in a place or house built for that purpose this was purposed in the mind of God before the world was & it was for this purpose that God designed to gather together the Jews oft but they would not it is for the same purpose that God gathers togethe the people in the last days to build unto the Lord an house to prepare them for the ordinances & endowment washings & anointings &c.[2]

Such special teachings and ordinances given in the Lord's temples were not and are not to be imparted to the world.

Speaking to His disciples, Jesus said, "It is given unto you to know the mysteries of the kingdom of heaven, but to them [the unbelieving multitude] it is not given" (Matthew 13:11; Luke 8:3). Jesus was able to teach his Apostles things that were kept from the world, including information about sacred ordinances. It is noteworthy that Paul saw Church leaders as "stewards of the mysteries of God" (1 Corinthians 4:1).

Nephi had "great desires to know of the mysteries of God." As a result of his pleadings to the Lord, the Lord visited him (1 Nephi 2:16). Nephi speaks of "having beheld great things" while "upon exceedingly high mountains" (2 Nephi 4:25). It seems likely that some of the things taught to him when he was on such mountains pertained to temple ordinances. In any case, Nephi was "bidden that [he] should not write them."

Regardless of their dispensation, all the inquiring faithful have been given special promises as to a recurring pattern: "For he that diligently seeketh shall find; and the mysteries of God shall be unfolded unto them, by the power of the Holy Ghost, as well in these times as in times of old, and as well in times of old as in times to come; wherefore, the course of the Lord is one eternal round" (1 Nephi 10:19).

These are special truths, therefore, which cannot be learned by logic; they must come from divine revelation. The Prophet Jacob's words affirm this: "Behold, great and marvelous are the works of the Lord. How unsearchable are the depths of the mysteries of him; and it is impossible that man should find out all his ways. And no man knoweth of his ways save it be revealed unto him; wherefore, brethren, despise not the revelations of God" (Jacob 4:8).

As noted previously, the precious brass plates contained some of the "mysteries of God" (Mosiah 1:3). These plates were essential, and therefore had "been kept and preserved by the hand of God" (Mosiah 1:5).

Those who are permitted to know the mysteries of God, however, "are laid under a strict command that they shall not impart only according to the portion of his word which he doth grant unto the children of men, according to the heed and diligence which they give unto him" (Alma 12:9). Depending upon our purity, our receptivity, and our desire for such knowledge, we too can come "to know the mysteries of God . . . in full" (Alma 12:10).

Those who know and care nothing concerning the simplifying and emancipating mysteries of God will experience instead the constraining "chains of hell" (Alma 12:11). These mysteries consist of truth-laden ordinances, but they are not fully efficacious if received barren of appropriate prerequisite behavior. Instead these ordinances and truths require that the would-be recipient "repenteth and exerciseth faith, and bringeth forth good works, and prayeth continually without ceasing—unto such it is given to know the mysteries of God" (Alma 26:22). Doing brings knowing (John 7:17).

Under way even now is the imparting to more and more worthy mortals of certain of these sacred things, things which have been kept and preserved to "go forth unto every nation, kindred, tongue, and people, that they shall know the mysteries of God contained thereon" (Alma 37:4). Such truths and ordinances do come gradually as well as individually. As one prophet observed, "These mysteries are not yet fully made known unto me; therefore I shall forbear" (Alma 37:11).

Given the importance of the mysteries of God (both ordinances and others), it is little wonder that we are counseled, "Seek not for riches but for wisdom; and, behold, the mysteries of God shall be unfolded unto you, and then shall you be made rich. Behold, he that hath eternal life is rich" (D&C 11:7).

Just as under certain conditions we sequentially "receive revelation upon revelation, knowledge upon knowledge" (D&C 42:61), there is also a particular sequence and succession of sacred ordinances.

First and always, however, we are to keep his commandments in order to receive the unfolding mysteries of the kingdom (D&C 63:23). And we must keep the covenants made in that process.

For all such unfolding the greater priesthood must be present, the priesthood which "administereth the gospel and holdeth the key of the mysteries of the kingdom" (D&C 84:19). When the higher priesthood was removed from ancient Israel, they were left without a portion of the higher ordinances of God (JST, Exodus 34:1–2; D&C 84:19–25). That priesthood, restored with the meridian dispensation, was subsequently lost to apostasy. With the bursting forth of the glorious gospel restoration that power was brought back by heavenly beings, never again to be taken from the earth.

In order to fulfill all righteousness, all must fulfill the same spiritual requirements for receiving the mysteries of the kingdom. Holy temples stand at the apogee of such divine disclosure.

While the temple is a place of service, work done there is not a substitute for Christian service in the outside world. It can be a powerful spur thereto, however, by reminding us of the need for sacrifice—not the giving of just our means but also of ourselves.

Temple attendance is not a guarantee that we will become

better, but it provides a powerful and pointed invitation to become better. The ways of the world receive constant reinforcement—should not the ways of heaven?

Temple work is not an escape from the world but a reinforcing of our need to better the world while preparing ourselves for another and far better world. Thus, being in the Lord's house can help us to be different from the world in order to make more difference in the world.

Temple work builds within us the spirit of gratitude for our past blessings even while preparing us to receive further blessings now and in the future.

The temple is a place where certain advanced doctrines are preached but, unlike those discussed in a Sunday School class, some of them are received by covenants. Since temple covenants are solemn and binding, a temple is thus no place to be in prematurely or unworthily.

To the unenlightened, advanced doctrines can be hard doctrines. Jesus' sermon at Capernaum contained hard doctrines about who He was, and then, "from that time many of his disciples went back, and walked no more with him" (John 6:66).

Sometimes, alas, it is like that for Church members who attend the temple before being properly prepared for it.

A temple provides a sanctuary away "from the madding crowd" and from the pressing cares of the world. Perhaps more than any other place, the temple reminds us that although as mortals we are in the world, we are not to be of the world. It helps us to function in the world without being overcome by the world. The more we come to the temple, the less likely we are to be overcome by the world. It is we, not the world, who are to do the overcoming (D&C 76:53).

Teachings in the temples take us beyond present time and space. We learn of special things therein, sometimes "things too wonderful for [us]" (Job 42:3) which require repeated attendance and prayer before meanings emerge.

With increased love for others, a major goal of the true Saint, life becomes larger as one's self becomes smaller in it, for then you and I "break out of this tiny and tawdry theatre in which [our] own little plot is always being played, and [we] . . . find [ourselves] under a freer sky, in a street full of splendid strangers."[3] One way to experience this enlargement is to frequent the house of the Lord. Duty may first bring us to the temple, but that duty can become a delight. The work we do is for those who are "splendid strangers"—but strangers only for now. Individuals who do the work for those "splendid strangers" now in the spirit world will become their true and everlasting friends.

Through a democracy of dress, temple attendance reminds us that God is no respecter of persons (Acts 10:34). The symbolic purity of white likewise reminds us that God is to have a pure people (D&C 100:16).

The center and pivot of everything worthwhile in the eternal sense, including the higher knowledge or mysteries our Father desires to share with the obedient, is Jesus Christ, our Savior and Redeemer. For those who have eyes to see, then, this is by intent a witnessing world. In fact both the world and the temple are designed to point us toward our Savior. Unfortunately many miss the connections because of "looking beyond the mark" (Jacob 4:14), as did some in ancient

Israel who failed to see that the law of Moses was a "typifying of [Christ]" (2 Nephi 11:4).

Ours is also a witnessing universe, whether in the Sacred Grove or a starlit night. "And behold, . . . all things are created and made to bear record of me" (Moses 6:63).

What is required for us to receive the mysteries, as is emphasized in the temple ceremony, is obedience to both the Lord's laws *and* His ordinances. This is much more than just a passive, intellectual attachment to some spiritual sayings, much more than a nodding approval of the Beatitudes.

When we think of consecration, Jesus again is our Perfect Exemplar. He gave His all. He sacrificed everything for us. He rightly asks that we make our much smaller sacrifice too: "Verily I say unto you, all among them who know their hearts are honest, and are broken, and their spirits contrite, and are willing to observe their covenants by sacrifice—yea, every sacrifice which I, the Lord, shall command—they are accepted of me" (D&C 97:8).

In our dispensation, what we place on the altar is not an animal but the animal in us!

With the glorious restoration of both pattern and substance, we can come to the temples *to learn:* "That [we] may be perfected in the understanding of [our] ministry, in theory, in principle, and in doctrine, in all things pertaining to the kingdom of God on the earth" (D&C 97:14).

And we come to the temple *to feel:* "That all people who shall enter upon the threshold of the Lord's house may feel thy power, and feel constrained to acknowledge that thou hast sanctified it, and that it is thy house, a place of thy holiness" (D&C 109:13).

And we come to the temple *to grow*: "That they may grow up in thee, and receive a fulness of the Holy Ghost, and be prepared to obtain every needful thing" (D&C 109:15).

And we come to the temple *to prepare to meet the Lord*: "Behold, the way for man is narrow, but it lieth in a straight course before him, and the keeper of the gate is the Holy One of Israel; and he employeth no servant there; and there is none other way save it be by the gate; for he cannot be deceived, for the Lord God is his name. And whoso knocketh, to him will he open" (2 Nephi 9:41–42).

As we ponder our almost incredible blessings in the outpouring of Restoration truths, and our individual potential to receive and comprehend yet more of the "mysteries," we should note the difference between on the one hand what the world tells us about ourselves, the universe, this planet, and Jesus, and on the other hand what the gospel, including the temple, tells us about these great realities. The gospel tells us such things as these:

> The earth rolls upon her wings, and the sun giveth his light by day, and the moon giveth her light by night, and the stars also give their light, as they roll upon their wings in their glory, in the midst of the power of God.
>
> Unto what shall I liken these kingdoms, that ye may understand?
>
> Behold, all these are kingdoms, and any man who hath seen any or the least of these hath seen God moving in his majesty and power (D&C 88:45–47).

> And worlds without number have I created; and I also created them for mine own purpose; and by the Son

I created them, which is mine Only Begotten (Moses 1:33).

For behold, this is my work and my glory—to bring to pass the immortality and eternal life of man (Moses 1:39).

The scriptures are laid before thee, yea, and all things denote there is a God; yea, even the earth, and all things that are upon the face of it, yea, and its motion, yea, and also all the planets which move in their regular form do witness that there is a Supreme Creator (Alma 30:44).

And behold, . . . all things are created and made to bear record of me, both things which are temporal, and things which are spiritual; things which are in the heavens above, and things which are on the earth, and things which are in the earth, and things which are under the earth, both above and beneath: all things bear record of me (Moses 6:63).

The world encourages us to pay attention to secular Caesars. The gospel tells us, however, that these Caesars come and go in an hour of pomp and show. It is God whom we should worship, and His Son, Jesus Christ. They have for us mortals a plan of salvation. God communicates His plan to mortals through angels and prophets:

And after God had appointed that these things should come unto man, behold, then he saw that it was expedient that man should know concerning the things whereof he had appointed unto them;

Therefore he sent angels to converse with them, who caused men to behold of his glory.

And they began from that time forth to call on his name; therefore God conversed with men, and made known unto them the plan of redemption, which had been prepared from the foundation of the world; and this he made known unto them according to their faith and repentance and their holy works (Alma 12:28–30).

And thus the Gospel began to be preached, from the beginning, being declared by holy angels sent forth from the presence of God, and by his own voice, and by the gift of the Holy Ghost (Moses 5:58).

The world concludes that man may spend his entire existence trying to persuade himself that life is not absurd. The gospel, on the other hand, tells us:

Man was also in the beginning with God. Intelligence, or the light of truth, was not created or made, neither indeed can be (D&C 93:29).

Adam fell that men might be; and men are, that they might have joy (2 Nephi 2:25).

Meanwhile, as the world measures status, we are so weak:

For ye see your calling, brethren, how that not many wise men after the flesh, not many mighty, not many noble, are called (1 Corinthians 1:26).

Yet the humble path to certain blessings is clear, and submission is essential. Joseph Smith said:

If a man gets a fullness of the priesthood of God he has to get it in the same way that Jesus Christ obtained it, and that was by keeping all the commandments and obeying all the ordinances of the house of the Lord. . . . There are a great many wise men and women too in our midst who are too wise to be taught; therefore they must die in their ignorance, and in the resurrection they will find their mistake.[4]

The meek are not "too wise to be taught."

This dispensation is thus one of fulness, yet it follows patterns in previous dispensations, as the Prophet Joseph taught:

[God's purpose] in the winding up scene of the last dispensation is, that all things pertaining to that dispensation should be conducted precisely in accordance with the preceeding dispensations.[5]

The pattern of inquiry persists under priesthood direction. Joseph Smith said:

I advise all to go on to perfection and search deeper and deeper into the mysteries of Godliness—a man can do nothing for himself unless God direct him in the right way, and the Priesthood is reserved for that purpose.[6]

Brigham Young made clear that to plain but faithful people, one day the "mysteries" will all be seen to be wonderfully simple:

If you could see things as they are, you would know that the whole plan of salvation, and all the revelations ever given to man on the earth are as plain as would be the remarks of an Elder, were he to stand here and talk about our every day business. . . . You may now be inclined to say, "O, this is too simple and child-like, we wish to hear the mysteries of the kingdoms of the Gods who have existed from eternity, and of all the kingdoms in which they will dwell; we desire to have these things portrayed to our understandings." Allow me to inform you that you are in the midst of it all now.[7]

Heber C. Kimball endorsed that concept:

If this people will do right there is nothing that will be a mystery to them; but those things which appeared the most mysterious will prove to be the most simple things in the world.[8]

Yet very solemn obligations accompany these ordinances and truths, as Brigham Young recognized:

Giving endowments to a great many proves their overthrow, through revealing things to them which they cannot keep.[9]

Plain and precious as these things are, they are essential. George Q. Cannon said:

Therefore it is essential that, if a people should be exalted unto the presence of God, they should have this Melchisedek or greater Priesthood, and the ordinances thereof, by the means of which they are to be prepared, or they shall be prepared to enter into the presence of God the Father, and endure His presence.[10]

The implications of these sacred things are vast, as Joseph Fielding Smith indicated:

> This Holy Priesthood, which is eternal, is the authority which prevails in all the universe. The ordinances of the gospel are made valid through its power, and without it the knowledge of God could not be made manifest. It is by this authority and through the ordinances that man is able to know of God. . . . Men may search and they may study, but they will never come to a knowledge of God until they receive the gospel and obtain light through the power of the priesthood and the ordinances of the gospel.[11]

These sacred blessings will lead us home, said Brigham Young:

> Your endowment is, to receive all those ordinances in the house of the Lord, which are necessary for you, after you have departed this life, to enable you to walk back to the presence of the Father.[12]

President Young's brief definition, if properly considered, cannot but swell the faithful and obedient heart with feelings of intense love and gratitude to God. This ascent to eternal life and the knowledge of all things is indeed the ultimate reward to those who willingly submit to his will in mortality as they daily strive to increase their righteousness—the true pattern for every genuine Latter-day Saint.

In that context, at the judgment bar of God we will "praise and adore at the mercy seat." We will not "stand all amazed"—instead we will kneel all amazed! Knowing the grandness and scope of God's work, we shall participate in that moment when every knee shall bow and every tongue confess that Jesus is the Christ (Philippians 2:10; D&C 76:110). Among those kneeling will be vilest of sinners, for whose sins Jesus also suffered (Mosiah 28:4). Among all the knees bending and the tongues confessing will be those of the leaders of all earthly religious movements, however diverse, good, or commendable those movements have been.

What we will feel on that occasion will be God's and Jesus' perfect love for us—not a scolding sternness but a profound kindness and immense tenderness. As these virtues flow from them toward us, many will feel the scalding shame of not having returned that love. As we feel their perfect love, we will confess that the justice and mercy of God are likewise perfect.

To stand approved of God at that great and last day— such is the challenge, such is the crucial nature of spiritual submissiveness while living in a tutoring world, "for in this world [our] joy is not full" (D&C 101:36). Body and spirit are not yet inseparably connected, death will come to us, yet we have been given profound promises.

If faithful and obedient in this good and beautiful world, we will inherit "a far better land of promise" (Alma 37:45), "a city whose builder and maker is God" (Hebrews 11:10). Within that city "are many mansions" (John 14:2–3) and no slums.

Paul wrote, "Eye hath not seen, nor ear heard, neither have entered into the heart of man [that is, we cannot even imagine], the things which God hath prepared for them that love him" (1 Corinthians 2:9).

The Lord delights to honor those who serve Him in righteousness (D&C 76:5).

The submissive will make it through to that final scene, for the word of God will lead the man and woman of Christ "in a straight and narrow course across that everlasting gulf of misery . . . and land their souls . . . at the right hand of God in the kingdom of heaven, to sit down with Abraham, and Isaac, and with Jacob, and with all our holy fathers" (Helaman 3:30) "who have been ever since the world began . . . to go no more out" (Alma 7:25).

Clearly, that will be a "better world . . . a place at the right hand of God" (Ether 12:4). The submissive, having overcome, will then be overcome after Father shares "all that [the] Father hath" (D&C 84:38). The faithful will hear those special words, "enter into the joy of [your] Lord" (D&C 51:9)! "They who have endured the crosses of the world, and despised the shame of it, they shall inherit the kingdom of God . . . and their joy shall be full forever" (2 Nephi 9:18).

What is the meaning of the promise that the arriving faithful will "go no more out"? Perhaps it is that time and space will no longer control us, as now. Even if we are "away on assignment," we will never again be "out," since we will be residing "in the presence of God . . . where all things . . . are manifest, past, present, and future, and are continually before the Lord" (D&C 130:7).

Meanwhile, here in mortality, we are given sure spiritual samplings of the world to come, real representations, if we will ponder and project.

Think of the most beautiful scenery you have ever witnessed, and yet realize that "eye hath not seen. . . ." Remember the most beautiful music you have heard, sounds which sent feelings soaring, and yet understand that "ear hath not heard."

Recall the finest moments of friendship, featuring nearly pure love. Reflect on joys, sorrows, and certitude shared. Yet the Creator of worlds, our best friend, has said, "I will call you friends, for you are my friends" (D&C 53:45). Our best moments of friendship are ahead of us.

Ponder those moments of keen, sudden insight, the flow of pure intelligence, such as Lamoni experienced when "light infused such joy into his soul" (Alma 19:6). Yet, "the day cometh [when] . . . all things shall be revealed . . . which ever have been . . . and which ever will be" (2 Nephi 27:11). The mysteries shall be ours, but shall be mysteries no more.

Reflect upon the occasions on which your conscience and integrity triumphed when, having done what was right and letting the consequences follow, you had a sure witness flood warmly into your soul and knew, like Enoch (Hebrews 11:5), that you had pleased Father.

Recollect the deepest moments of marital and familial joy, whether in rejoicings, reunions, or reconciliations, when "because of the great goodness of God" there was a "gushing out of many tears" (3 Nephi 4:33); when your "heart [was] brim with joy" (Alma 26:11). Yet this was but a foretaste of the ultimate homecoming, when our cups will not only be brim but will run over without ceasing.

The above are sure samplings but only samplings, like representative post cards from that far better world, telling us, in Jacob's words, of "things as they really will be" (Jacob 4:13).

And what price do we pay for this great reward? In King Benjamin's words, putting off the natural man, yielding to the

Holy Spirit, becoming a saint through the Atonement, and becoming "as a child, submissive, meek, humble, patient, full of love, willing to submit to all things which the Lord seeth fit to inflict upon [us], even as a child doth submit to his father."

Our great Example showed us the pattern by His life, and then in his most desperate hour (Luke 22:41–43) summed up in five words for all time the way of both the Master and His disciple:

"Not my will, but thine."

Notes and References

CHAPTER 1: "AS OBEDIENT CHILDREN"

1. Joseph Smith, *Teachings of the Prophet Joseph Smith*, sel. Joseph Fielding Smith (Salt Lake City: Deseret Book Company, 1976), p. 309.

2. Andrew F. Ehat and Lyndon W. Cook, eds., *The Words of Joseph Smith* (Provo: Religious Studies Center, Brigham Young University, 1980), p. 347.

3. Bertrand Russell, "A Free Man's Worship," in *Mysticism and Logic and Other Essays* (London: George Allen and Unwin Ltd., 1950), p. 57.

4. *George MacDonald: An Anthology*, C. S. Lewis, ed. (New York: Macmillan Publishing Co., Inc., 1978), p. 88.

5. PBS production of Ford Madox Ford's *The Good Soldier*.

6. *Teachings of the Prophet Joseph Smith*, pp. 255–256.

7. Lucy Maude Montgomery, *Anne of Green Gables* (New York: Avenel Books, 1985), pp. xiii-xiv.

CHAPTER 2: "THE GREAT QUESTION"

1. These books include: Wars of the Lord, Jasher, more from Samuel, the Acts of Solomon, the book of Nathan, Shemaiah,

Ahijah, Iddo, Jehu, the Sayings of the Seers, at least two epistles of Paul, the book of Enoch, Ezias, Neum, Adam's book of remembrance, Zenos, Zenock, and Gad the Seer.

Apparently, we only have a portion of certain prophecies from Jacob, or Israel, while we have extensive prophecies by Joseph in Egypt (2 Nephi 3:1–25 and 4:1–2; JST, Genesis 50:24–37; Alma 46:24–26). This suggests the possibility of further prophecies by both these prophets which are yet to come to light.

2. Joseph Smith said of the title page of the Book of Mormon: "The title-page of the Book of Mormon is a literal translation, taken from the very last leaf, on the left hand side of the collection or book of plates . . . and . . . said title-page is not by any means a modern composition, either of mine or of any other man who has lived or does live in this generation." (Joseph Smith, *Teachings of the Prophet Joseph Smith*, sel. Joseph Fielding Smith [Salt Lake City: Deseret Book Company, 1976], p. 7.)

3. C. S. Lewis, *The Last Battle* (New York: The Macmillan Company, 1956), p. 140.

4. Furthermore, too few people follow the counsel of Moroni regarding the book's substance: "Condemn me not because of mine imperfection, neither my father, because of his imperfection, neither them who have written before him; but rather give thanks to God that he hath made manifest unto you our imperfections, that ye may learn to be more wise than we have been" (Mormon 9:31).

5. Michael Harrington, *The Politics at God's Funeral* (New York: Holt, Rinehart and Winston, 1983), pp. 153, 164.

6. Penelope Fitzgerald, *The Knox Brothers* (New York: Coward, McCann & Geoghegan, Inc., 1977), pp. 106–107.

7. Percy Bysshe Shelley, *The Complete Works of Shelley* (Boston: Houghton Mifflin Co., 1901), p. 356.

8. *Teachings of the Prophet Joseph Smith*, p. 383.

Chapter 3: "A Marvellous Work"

1. Neal A. Maxwell, *But for a Small Moment* (Salt Lake City: Bookcraft, 1986), p. 54.

2. Andrew F. Ehat and Lyndon W. Cook, eds., *The Words of Joseph Smith* (Provo: Religious Studies Center, Brigham Young University, 1980), p. 120.

3. Joseph Fielding Smith, *Answers to Gospel Questions*, vol. 2 (Salt Lake City: Deseret Book Company, 1958), pp. 121–122.

4. William D. Edwards, MD; Wesley J. Gabel, MDiv; Floyd E. Hosmer, MS, AMI, "On the Physical Death of Jesus Christ," *Journal of the American Medical Association* 255 (March 21, 1986): 1458–1463.

Chapter 4: "The Infinite Atonement"

1. Bruce R. McConkie, *Mormon Doctrine* (Salt Lake City: Bookcraft, 1979), pp. 64–66.

2. John Taylor, *The Mediation and Atonement* (Salt Lake City: Deseret News, 1882), p. 77.

3. Marion G. Romney, "Jesus Christ, Lord of the Universe," *Improvement Era*, November 1968, p. 49.

Chapter 5: "Faith Unto Repentance"

1. Marion G. Romney, Monterrey Mexico Area Conference, February 19 and 20, 1977 (Salt Lake City: The Church of Jesus Christ of Latter-day Saints, 1978), p. 10.

2. *George MacDonald: An Anthology*, C. S. Lewis, ed. (New York: Macmillan Publishing Co., Inc., 1978), p. 28.

3. *George MacDonald: An Anthology*, p. 110.

4. Michael Harrington, *The Politics at God's Funeral* (New York: Holt, Reinhart, Winston, 1983), p. 3.

5. Andrew F. Ehat and Lyndon W. Cook, *The Words of Joseph*

Smith (Provo: Religious Studies Center, Brigham Young University, 1980), p. 237.

6. *George MacDonald: An Anthology*, p. 32.

7. Joseph Smith, *Teachings of the Prophet Joseph Smith*, sel. Joseph Fielding Smith (Salt Lake City: Deseret Book Company, 1976), p. 87.

8. *George MacDonald: An Anthology*, p. 3.

9. *The Words of Joseph Smith*, p. 107.

10. *The Words of Joseph Smith*, p. 115.

11. *The Words of Joseph Smith*, p. 123.

12. *The Words of Joseph Smith*, p. 124.

13. *George MacDonald: An Anthology*, p. 19.

14. *George MacDonald: An Anthology*, pp. 25–26.

15. *George MacDonald: An Anthology*, p.69.

16. *Teachings of the Prophet Joseph Smith*, p. 51.

17. Walt Harrington, "Revenge of the Dupes," *The Washington Post Magazine*, December 27, 1987, pp. 18–19.

18. Walt Harrington, "Revenge of the Dupes," p. 19.

19. Robert Bolt, *A Man for All Seasons* (New York: Random House, 1960), p. 66.

CHAPTER 6: "WILLING TO SUBMIT"

1. "I Stand All Amazed," *Hymns*, no. 193.

2. From "The Humanist Manifesto II," *The Humanist*, September-October, 1973, p. 2, as quoted by Brian J. Fogg in "The Gospel and Applied Christianity," *The Student Review*, Dec. 9, 1987, p. 32.

3. George MacDonald, "That Holy Thing," *Masterpieces of Religious Verse*, James Dalton Morrison, ed. (New York: Harper and Brothers Publishers, 1948), p. 144.

4. James Thomas Flexner, *Washington: The Indispensable Man* (Boston: Little, Brown and Company, 1974), pp. 28, 31, 38.

5. *Washington: The Indispensable Man*, p. xvi.

6. *Interpreter's Dictionary of the Bible* (New York: Abingdon Press, 1962), 3:580.

7. Joseph Smith, *Teachings of the Prophet Joseph Smith*, sel. Joseph Fielding Smith (Salt Lake City: Deseret Book Company, 1976), p. 311.

8. See Donald Q. Cannon and Lyndon W. Cook, eds., *Far West Record: Minutes of The Church of Jesus Christ of Latter-day Saints: 1830–1844* (Salt Lake City: Deseret Book Company, 1983), p. 286.

9. *Teachings of the Prophet Joseph Smith*, p. 357.

10. *Teachings of the Prophet Joseph Smith*, p. 67.

11. Gordon B. Hinckley, "Taking the Gospel to Britain: A Declaration of Vision, Faith, Courage, and Truth," *Ensign*, July 1987, p. 7.

12. Thomas S. Monson, "Courage Counts," *Ensign*, November 1986, pp. 41–42.

13. Edward L. Kimball and Andrew E. Kimball, *Spencer W. Kimball* (Salt Lake City: Bookcraft, 1977), pp. 311–312.

CHAPTER 7: "IF THOU ENDURE WELL"

1. *Familiar Quotations,* 14th ed., John Bartlett, comp. (London: Macmillan, 1968), pp. 247, 355, 387, 604, 883.

2. *Familiar Quotations*, p. 679.

3. *Familiar Quotations*, p. 679.

4. *Familiar Quotations,* p. 661.

5. C. S. Lewis, *The Weight of Glory* (Grand Rapids: The William B. Eerdmans Publishing Company, 1965), p. 14.

6. Joseph Smith, *Lectures on Faith* (Salt Lake City: Deseret Book, 1985), 3:5.

7. *Lectures on Faith* 6:4.

CHAPTER 8: "THE MYSTERIES OF THE KINGDOM"

1. Andrew F. Ehat and Lyndon W. Cook, eds., *The Words of Joseph Smith* (Provo: Religious Studies Center, Brigham Young University, 1980), p. 84, note 13.

2. *The Words of Joseph Smith,* pp. 212–213.

3. G.K. Chesterton, *Orthodoxy* (New York: Doubleday & Company, 1959), p. 21.

4. Joseph Smith, *Teachings of the Prophet Joseph Smith,* sel. Joseph Fielding Smith (Salt Lake City: Deseret Book Company, 1976), pp. 308–309.

5. *The Words of Joseph Smith,* p. 39.

6. *The Words of Joseph Smith,* p. 366.

7. Brigham Young, *Journal of Discourses,* 26 vols. (London: Latter-day Saints' Book Depot, 1854–86), 3:336.

8. Heber C. Kimball, *Journal of Discourses,* 3:112.

9. Brigham Young, *Journal of Discourses,* 4:372.

10. George Q. Cannon, *Journal of Discourses,* 25:292.

11. Joseph Fielding Smith, Conference Report, April 1967, pp.97–98.

12. Brigham Young, *Journal of Discourses,* 2:31.

Index

About the Author

Elder Neal A. Maxwell, who previously served as executive vice president at the University of Utah and as Commissioner of Education for The Church of Jesus Christ of Latter-day Saints, was sustained as an Assistant to the Twelve in 1974 and called to the Quorum of the Twelve Apostles in 1981. A well-beloved speaker and author, he wrote more than twenty-five books, including *Whom the Lord Loveth, The Promise of Discipleship, One More Strain of Praise, If Thou Endure It Well,* and *All These Things Shall Give Thee Experience.* Elder Maxwell passed away July 21, 2004. He and his wife, Colleen Hinckley Maxwell, have four children and twenty-four grandchildren.